A TREASURY OF WITCHCRAFT AND DEVILRY

A Primer of the Occult

MARIE GUPTA and FRAN BRANDON

JONATHAN DAVID PUBLISHERS
MIDDLE VILLAGE, N.Y. 11379

A TREASURY OF WITCHCRAFT AND DEVILRY
by
MARIE GUPTA and FRAN BRANDON

Address all inquiries to:

JONATHAN DAVID PUBLISHERS
Middle Village, New York 11379

Library of Congress Cataloging in Publication Data

Gupta, Marie.
A treasury of witchcraft and devilry.

1. Witchcraft. 2. Demonology. 3. Ghosts. 4. Occult sciences. I. Brandon, Frances Sweeney, joint author. II. Title.
BF1566.G86 133 74-6571

ISBN: 978-0-8246-0190-4

PRINTED IN THE UNITED STATES OF AMERICA

TABLE OF CONTENTS

Introduction

IT IS WISE that we think of the occult in a serious vein, because it is impossible to be a thinking person and to ignore it. In this book we shall explore the ways in which people have attuned themselves to the rhythm of that dark stream which flows somewhere in the back of the mind, and evokes elusive shadows and memories that have been forgotten or lost.

Jung called this feeling "racial memory," a type of recollection that operates in terms of symbols. It can only be reached by "hushing the unquiet mind" and descending to deeper levels of awareness. Or, in the words of an old proverb:

> If ye would clear the path to will,
> Make certain that the mind be still.

The Irish poet, Yeats, suggested that magic powers are achieved by "touching the subliminal depths" to create symbols. He said, "I cannot now think symbols less than the greatest of all powers, whether they are used consciously by the masters of magic or half-unconsciously by their successors, the poet, the musician, and the artist."

The truly great musician, poet, and artist are also people of power. Like the genuine adepts of the occult, they have been able to transcend themselves and to draw power from an elemental source.

The Spanish word *duende* is the most apt expression of the power that is felt in the occult. Goethe defines *duende* as "a mysterious power that everyone feels but that no philosopher has explained."

The Spanish poet Garcia Lorca explains *duende* in these terms:

> All that has dark sounds had *duende*. It is not a matter of ability, but of a living form of blood, of ancient culture, of creative action. To help us seek the *duende*, there is neither map nor discipline. All one knows is that it turns the blood to powdered glass, that it exhausts, that it rejects all the sweet geometry one has learned, that it breaks with all styles.

The powers which we discuss in this book are the powers of witches, sorcerers, and devils. Broadly speaking, these powers are divination and control. By divination, we mean the use of special insight to gain knowledge of a person's character, of the future, or of the spirit world. The control of which we speak is the ability of certain individuals to make others follow their will and the ability to control oneself in defiance of involuntary natural reactions.

The incidents which we use to illustrate these powers have been chosen for their dramatic interest. Naturally, we do not believe that all incidents which purport to be occult are genuinely so. It is important, though often difficult, to separate the fraudulent imitators from the genuine possessors of psychic power. We have included many examples of what is known as "general occult lore," the notions from which superstition and tradition are woven.

We, the authors, are neither witches nor Satanists. We prefer to call ourselves students of the occult who are still learning, for there is always more to be learned. In this book, we have tried to present an interesting and impartial view of various facets of witchcraft, devils, and other occult lore.

The body of knowledge concerning witches and devils is so vast, and in many cases so subjective, that no work on the subject can claim to be exhaustive or definitive. Our purpose, then, is to allow the reader a glimpse into this shadowy and fascinating world which will hopefully bring him a step closer to an understanding of the hidden powers.

A TREASURY OF WITCHCRAFT AND DEVILRY

Méphistophélès, the popular sophisticated devil. From a pen drawing in a French occult manuscript, *La Magie Noire,* Paris, nineteenth century.

PART I

1. The Emergence of Witchcraft

Prehistoric Beginnings

THE HISTORY OF witchcraft can be traced to the days of the caveman and belongs as much in the province of the anthropologist as the occultist. Since there are no written records of that time, anthropologists must attempt to reconstruct the activities of these very ancient people from relics, cave paintings, and their knowledge of the nature of mankind. Pennethorne Hughes states in *Witchcraft* that witchcraft almost everywhere was derived mainly from a combination of local fertility rites and later magical practices which filtered into the various countries from Egypt. These influences were modified by the distinctive characteristics of each culture.

Before witchcraft could emerge, man needed to have a desire to interact with others. The fear of being alone is a primitive one, and it was not long before primitive man found himself making sympathetic movements in response to the movements of another human being. One would raise his hand, the other would raise his hand in response, and a bond was created between them.

The next step was the mime, in which one man would act out a past experience, such as the hunt of the previous day. Later, he might act out what he could expect to do in the next day's hunt. Others would join him, and the group would enact a communal mime.

A series of sympathetic movements combined with communal mime led to the dance, which was a necessary step in the growth of magic and eventually of religion. The dance became a protection, an activity in which the individual could lose his sense of separateness and merge into the pattern of the group.

As the structure of the dance expanded, the dancers would lose themselves in the rhythm, entering a trance-like state which merged them all into a sense of tribal consciousness rather than of self-consciousness. The unity which they achieved was the beginning of group religion, and the eventual emergence of a leader of the dance was the beginning of the idea of priesthood.

Primitive art was another form of group magic. As a symbol which had meaning to a group, a drawn picture was also a means of evoking tribal consciousness.

Sympathetic magic also began to be practiced, in which a man would drink the blood of his victim to acquire the dead man's courage or strength. He would wear the horns of a stag to acquire the animal's speed and grace or the fur of an animal to gain its fierceness. The objects used in sympathetic magic were eventually incorporated into the dance, which became more ritualistic and symbolistic.

The Little People

As man moved out of the Neolithic Age and into the Iron Age, the race of smaller people who were remnants of Neolithic man inspired the idea of little magic people in northern and western Europe. These early spirits were known to be malicious and frightening. They were feared by the more advanced groups and thus became the forerunners of the hobgoblins, gnomes, and trolls; the concept of good fairies and elves had not yet emerged. As they roamed the forests hunting for prey, they were held responsible for accidents which occured in the forest, for drownings, diseases, and the death of animals. The small people feared only iron, the mysterious substance of which weapons could be made.

Folk Witches and Fairies

From their belief in the little people, each country developed itslegendary folk witches and fairies; it was the magic of these imaginary beings which eventually became witchcraft.

In Germany, Holda was known as the earth mother who was responsible for fertility and growing things. Grunhutl the green huntsman, would hunt in the company of witches.

England had a similar figure, known as Herne the Hunter, who was feared for his wickedness. From England we also hear of Rob Roy, the mountain satyr who dressed in goatskin. The well-known Robin Hood and Maid Marian have caused speculation among students of witchcraft as to whether or not these woodland people were actually members of a witch's coven or group. However, it is unlikely that organized witchcraft existed at that time; more probably, Robin Hood and Maid Marian followed what William Wood refers to as *la vecchia religione,* which was not actually a religion, but a way of life which included herb lore and animism.

In France, Dusius was the devil and fertility god, similar to Rob Roy and to the Greek Pan, who was responsible for various pranks and mischief. Another French legend tells of Melusine of Lusignan, the fairy who was a child of the Devil. As a symbol of change, she was required to walk on serpents' legs every seventh night.

The gypsies, whose witchcraft traditions were in some ways similar to the other Europeans', also had their legendary fairies and giants. These are discussed in the chapter on gypsy witchcraft. It is interesting to note that certain prototypes, such as the satyr, the malevolent hunter, and the earth mother, are represented in every culture.

Animism and Herb Lore

It has already been mentioned that *la vecchia religione* was not truly a religion. It simply was a term which encompassed certain things which people did in reaction to an instinctive feeling that powers exist which cannot be seen. Certainly it was an important stage in the development of witchcraft.

Animism, which is one facet of this stage, developed as man began to wonder about the cause of natural occurrences such as lightning, thunder, floods, diseases, and the growth of plants. Unable to conceive a scientific explanation, he began to believe in spirits which inhabited trees, rivers, the earth, and all other familiar things.

To make life go smoothly, he found it necessary to encourage the benevolent spirits and drive away or pacify the evil ones. Stones, trees, and wells were worshiped, and the practice of sacrifice was begun as a means of satisfying the spirits. Eventually this grew into the idea of sacrifice to gods or demons.

Herb lore also developed in a natural way as people found by trial and error that certain plants caused dramatic effects when eaten or made into a poultice. Certain persons were especially skilled in the preparation and use of these herbs. They became the herbalists who sold charms and potions to heal sickness or ensure success in love.

As herb lore became a part of *la vecchia religione,* the herbalists developed rituals for the gathering of herbs. Certain herbs were to be gathered by moonlight; others had to be picked only on designated days. To make the magic of the herbs more effective, incantations were said during their preparation and use. Herb lore thus evolved into an early form of witchcraft.

Other Early Witches

The Celtic Druids, the Delphic Oracles, and the Dionysians of Thrace were early groups whose activities and characteristics were later attributed to witches. In early Rome, witches practiced spells using effigies, as witches around the world still do today.

The Druids were members of an early Celtic religion. Their reputation endowed them with all the magic of witches—the casting of lethal spells, the ability to become invisible, control over the elements, and the sacrifice of humans and animals. They were a cruel sect who practiced their rites in the depths of the woods.

The legendary high priestess of the Druids, known as Herla, Hertha, or Velleda, was characterized by the distaff which she carried. This scepter was entwined with black and white threads symbolizing the Fates.

In Greece, the Delphic Oracles were among the early diviners. They would inhale intoxicating vapours which would enable them to reach a trance state and make prophetic statements.

The Dionysian cult of Thrace consisted of worshipers of sensual pleasure. Their orgiastic dancing, drinking, brawling, copulating, and choral singing formed a part of the later Sabbat, or ritual gathering of witches.

The Roman poet Horace describes an incident concerning witches in the Equiline cemetery:

> At the new moon they steal into it [the cemetery] to gather bones and noxious herbs, their feet bare, their hair loose, and their soles tucked in. Making a hollow in the ground, they rend a black lamb over it to summon the dead. They take two images—a larger one of wool [representing a witch] and a smaller one of wax [representing the person to be bewitched or punished]. The moon turns red, hell hounds and snakes glide over the spot. Then they bury the muzzle of a wolf and a snake's tooth and burn the waxen images.

These witches were working a necromantic spell, which calls upon the assistance of the spirits of the dead. Necromancy and murder by magical means were punishable crimes in the Rome of Horace's time.

Sorcerers

The word "sorcerer" comes from the Latin word *sors* meaning "spell." The sorcerers practiced various kinds of spells for serious purposes. Most sorcerers were men who worked alone and in secrecy. Some were also alchemists, who attempted to convert the base metals to gold and silver.

Many of these sorcerers were of the type known as intellectual sorcerers, who flourished during the Middle Ages in Germany, Hungary, and Flanders. The typical intellectual sorcerer was an old man who had secluded himself from the rest of the town. He was often rumored to be rich and to have a pretty daughter who was very innocent and seen only at Mass. He would study the *Cabala,* the ancient Hebrew book of mysticism, to learn about secret pentacles, magic symbols, and the magic circle, which was necessary to most of his spells. This type of sorcerer was also familiar with astrology, alchemy, and the making of robots. Doctor Faust was typical of the intellectual sorcerer.

Sorcerers could invoke the curse of hell on their enemies,

call up the Devil or demons, summon spirits, read tarot cards or palms, and obtain material benefits for those who had made a pact with the Devil.

Some famous sorcerers who practiced alchemy and divination were the monks Roger Bacon and Albertus Magnus; the Popes Leo the Great, Honorius, and Silvester II; and the monarchs Henri III, Catherine de Medici, and King Richard. King Richard had a demon mother and was known to be a sorcerer because he was humpbacked and had a full set of teeth before he was six months old.

Also included among sorcerers are the ninth-century English weather wizards. These wizards could bring on storms or protect the inhabitants of their region from treacherous weather conditions. Female weather wizards lived on the Isle of Man. They controlled the weather by tying knots in a length of cord. As each knot was untied, the wind would rise in intensity.

Similar to the weather witches were the Finnish witches, who would offer to sell sailors the wind bound up in three knots of rope. Untying the first knot would cause a breeze, untying the second would create a gale, and untying the third would unleash a tempest.

In Estonia, witches would thrust a knife into a block of wood from the direction in which they wanted the wind to blow.

Scottish witches raised the wind by dipping a rag in a brook and beating it on a square stone while chanting:

> Upon this stone I knock a rag
> To raise the wind in the lady's name.
> It shall not lie or cease or die
> Until I please again.

Witches of England would whistle up the wind. By the first light of dawn, they would face the direction from which the wind was to come and blow three long, clear whistles between the first and fourth fingers of the right hand.

Witchcraft Emerges

During the late Middle Ages and the Renaissance, when many European countries were in the process of changing from a pagan to a Christian way of life, witchcraft was practiced by those who still clung to the animistic beliefs and fertility cults of former times. The devil whom they worshiped took the form of various animals. He resembled the pagan gods or satyrs rather than the Christianized devil who became the symbol of evil.

The witches of these times were believed to prophesy, cast spells, raise storms, change shape, fly, and perform other feats of power. For instance, love and marriage among ordinary mortals often depended upon magic and witchcraft. Witches could give a woman a ring to blind her husband to her infidelity or give the husband an aphrodisiac to increase his interest in his wife. Love philtres were sought by those whose love was unrequited. A man could be made impotent by a process known as ligature, in which knots were tied in a thread. In some parts of Europe, ligature was considered sufficient grounds for divorce.

As Christianity spread and the pressure grew to conform to its ways, witches adopted practices which were parodies of Christian rituals. This came to be known as black magic.

The Pact with the Devil

An important aspect of black, or malevolent, witchcraft is the pact with the Devil. The idea of such a pact is thought to have originated in Byzantium, then spread into Europe.

The Bible contains a reference in Isaiah 28:15 which might be interpreted as a forerunner of the pact:

> We have made a covenant with death, and with Sheol [Hell] we have an agreement.

St. Augustine condemned the pact:

> Therefore all superstitions of this kind. arising out of damnable consorting of men and demons as if formed by a faithless pact of friendship are to be intrinsically repudiated.

The pact was a written contract, usually signed in blood. To bind the pact, the witch would receive a witch's mark, also known as the mark of the Devil. This mark would be branded on the witch's body, sometimes in red, sometimes in blue. The witch's mark was considered to be invulnerable to pain or injury.

In the pact, the witches would promise to:

1. repudiate God
2. renounce the Christian faith
3. tread or spit upon the cross and commit obscenities with it
4. curse, blaspheme, and provoke God
5. despise the seven sacraments
6. accept baptism by Satan in a new name
7. break the fast on fast days
8. fast on feast days
9. observe and keep all of the Devil's commandments
10. give body and soul to the Devil
11. procure as many new members as possible
12. steal unbaptized children to make ointments (at least one child per witch each month)
13. give all their offspring to the devil without baptism
14. burn all their children when they had sacrificed them
15. eat the flesh and drink the blood of humans
16. kill men with poison
17. kill men's cattle
18. bewitch men's corn
19. bring hunger and barrenness to the countyside
20. ride and fly in the air
21. bring storms and tempests
22. cause men, women, or animals to be barren
23. make horses kick and throw their riders
24. make themselves invulnerable to torture
25. create terror in humans
26. see hidden things
27. predict the future
28. kill with lightning and thunder
29. make men love or hate
30. take away men's courage
31. make women miscarry
32. kill with looks
33. sink ships

From the confessions made by witches during the witch trials of the sixteenth and seventeenth centuries, some general ideas were formed concerning the way in which the Devil recruited women to become witches.

In 1616, a young woman named Elspeth Reoch of Orkney confessed that she had made the Devil's acquaintance at the age of twelve. Two men had approached her while she was waiting for a ferry to cross the lake. One was dressed in green tartan plaid, the other in black. The one in plaid told Elspeth that she was very pretty and that he would teach her to know and see whatever she should desire. She confessed at the trial that she had lain with the man in black, whom she called the "fairy man," and bore him a child.

In 1633, another woman on trial, Margaret Johnson, recalled that the Devil had appeared to her also in the shape of a man. He called himself Mamillion and made her believe that he was a god.

Other confessions described a meeting with a soft-spoken man dressed in black, green, or gray. He was sometimes young, sometimes old, but always sophisticated and fashionably dressed. Sometimes he rode a horse, at other times he walked on cloven feet. He often approached young girls and taught them how to ride to the Sabbat.

The Sabbat

The Sabbat, or Sabbath, was the ritual gathering at which witches were said to worship Satan, perform lewd and macabre acts, and desecrate Christian rites. There is no record of the Sabbat before the fourteenth century, and it is uncertain whether such a ritual actually existed. Possibly the idea of a ceremony which parodied the Church was imagined by the Inquisitors based on various isolated practices. The belief in the dance of the Sabbat may have originated from the nocturnal dancing of groups of serfs. Those who practiced black magic in those times were often the poor, the old, or the misfits who felt oppressed by the rigid and dogmatic confines of the Church. Perhaps many of these oppressed persons gathered in groups and later, under pressure from the Inquisition, actually imagined that they had participated in the bizarre ritual of the Sabbat.

Traditionally, witches were known to fly to the Sabbat on brooms, donkeys, goats, cats, or even the Devil in animal form. Their powers of flight were acquired by rubbing on themselves a vile-smelling ointment. Many of these ointments contained soot to cause invisibility, the fat of a newborn baby, the blood of a bat, various harmless herbs, hemlock, and the deadly nightshade, which contains belladonna. The last two ingredients, which in larger doses will cause death, if taken in a small dose will produce a nervous or delirious excitement.

These ingredients were thought to be the secret of the flight to which so many accused witches testified with complete sincerity. Apparently, under the influence of the stimulating herbs, the witches would experience a sensation of flying and would actually believe themselves to be moving through the air.

There have been many representations of witches in flight; these often show the witch sitting backwards on her mount. Before the seventeenth century, witches were shown riding on a broom whose head pointed downward. After the seventeenth century, the head pointed upward, sometimes with a candle stuck in it.

A witch could not leave for the Sabbat through the doorway, but had to go through a keyhole or chimney. There is a belief that a witch must enter a building by the opening through which she left it.

As in the pact and the flight, details of the Sabbat came to light through the questioning of the Inquisitors. The Sabbat would begin with the adoration of Satan, who would appear as a huge black man or he-goat. The witches would offer him blue-flamed candles and kiss his back, shoulders, and buttocks. Then the circular dance would begin, in which the witches and demons danced back to back to avoid recognition. As the dance became more frenzied, the dancers would break into couples which intermingled in orgies.

The next event of the Sabbat was the banquet, at which the main course was often a dead child. With the meal, the witches drank wine and water, but salt was never permitted. Salt is anathema to the devil because it symbolizes immortality and is used in holy water.

The food itself would have no flavor and the meat was always horseflesh or human flesh. The meal also had a strange quality of not filling the stomach; the witches would finish the meal as hungry as when they began. Grace was said after the meal, parodying and blaspheming Christian prayer and hailing Satan as author and preserver of all things.

After the meal, the business part of the meeting would begin. The witches would describe to Satan the evil deeds they had committed since the previous meeting. Satan would praise those who has been especially evil and mock those who had been remiss in fulfilling their pact. He would conclude by giving a speech meant to inspire the witches to further malice. Always, he would cry out the words: "Revenge yourselves or you shall die!"

Together the group of witches would cause a hailstorm to precede the parody of the celebration of Mass. At this Black Mass, the participants renounced God and the sacraments and blasphemed God, the Virgin Mary, and the Saints. They would renew their oaths of allegiance to the Devil and deny all hope of heaven. The Black Mass would make use of a black radish as the host and false holy water.

At the close of the Mass, the devil would take the form of a he-goat which was steadily consumed by fire. The witches would collect the ashes to use in spells.

Witches' Familiars

Each witch had as a companion a familiar spirit in the shape of an animal. Any animal could be a familiar, but the most commonly known were cats, toads, or owls. These familiars would aid the witches in casting spells and inform them of the time and place of each meeting. Some witches rode to the Sabbat meeting on the backs of their familiars.

At the Salem witch trials one of the defendants was accused of keeping a small yellow bird as a familiar.

In nineteenth century Scotland, a Great Auk was burned as a witch.

The word "mascot" derives from the Portuguese *mascotto* meaning "witchcraft," probably because of the animal familiars.

Witches' Transformations

Witches were supposedly capable of transforming themselves into animals. A witch might transform herself into an animal in order to go to the Sabbat despite obstacles. During the Inquisition, guards were cautioned to be alert against the possibility of witches escaping by this means.

The most dramatic type of transformation that a witch could make was the transformation into a werewolf. This type of transformation is known as *lycanthropy*. Strange stories were told of werewolves encountered in the forests of Europe.

In *Witchcraft: The Story of Man's Quest for Supernatural Power,* Eric Maple tells of the werewolves of Poligny, a village near the Swiss border of France. A traveler through that region was attacked by a wolf. To defend himself, he struck the animal with a sword and succeeded in driving it away.

Following the injured wolf, the traveler found himself at the cottage of a man named Michael Verdung. Verdung was at that moment having some sword-cuts bandaged by his wife. The traveler reported his findings, and Verdung and three accomplices were arrested. They were found guilty of a pact with Satan, cannabalism, and intercourse with she-wolves. All were burned.

Boguet's *Discours Exécrable des Sorciers,* a seventeenth-century work, tells a story of a hunter who was attacked by a wolf in the mountains. The hunter cut off the wolf's paw and the animal fled in pain. The man kept the paw and later showed it to his friend, a young nobleman. When he pulled the paw from his pocket, he saw that it had become a woman's hand with a ring on it. The young nobleman recognized the ring as one belonging to his wife. When he confronted her, he saw that her hand was bandaged. He then denounced her as a witch.

The White Witches of the Eighteenth Century

By the end of the seventeenth century, the persecution of witches had ended and black witches were becoming fewer. The witches of the eighteenth century were the white witches who, like the early herbalists, dealt mainly in healing and love potions.

White witches had existed during the centuries of black witch persecution. Their function then had been to discover the black witches and denounce them, and to protect individuals against black witchcraft.

Many of these white witches claimed to be seventh sons or seventh daughters, which meant that their powers were inherited. A seventh daughter of a seventh daughter was the most powerful type of white witch.

In the British Isles, white witches were consulted by the superstitious poor. In Scotland, the seventh daughters of seventh daughters were called spae-wives and served as fortune-tellers.

As the years passed, the descendants of witches died out and the practice of witchcraft dwindled. Most modern witches are not descendants of witches and have formed their ideas of witchcraft more from books on the subject than from lore handed down through many generations.

2. The Persecution of Witches and Sorcerers

Laws against Witchcraft

THE EARLIEST INJUNCTION against witches is found in the biblical command: "Thou shalt not suffer a witch to live" (Exodus 22:18). Modern scholars, however, contend that the word translated as "witch" actually means "poisoner" and that the persons referred to as witches in the Bible were either sorcerers or, in the case of the witch of Endor, mediums. Yet the fear of those beings who could perform supernatural feats was already implanted. The anti-witchcraft laws of many countries testify to that fear.

The earlier laws were relatively lenient. However, as the traditional concept of the witch was solidified, the fear increased and the laws became more strict until they reached a peak of hysteria during the Inquisition. France and England were the countries most concerned with the persecution of witches. Other European countries adopted similar laws, but their attack on witches was less intense and less sustained. Early Salic law stated that a witch who had eaten man's flesh must pay 200 sous. A person who accused another of sorcery without proof must pay 62½ gold sous.

In 363, the Ecclesiastical Council of Laodicea decreed that sorcerers should be driven out of the land and fined.

In 506, the Council of Agde in Languedoc excommunicated vampires, sorcerers, and poisoners.

In 541, the Council at Orleans forbade divination.

In 589, the Council of Narbonne ordered sorcerers to be sold as slaves.

In 685, Theodore, Archbishop of Canterbury, declared it sinful to sacrifice to demons, to eat or drink in a heathen temple, or to dress as a stag or bull.

In 690, Wihtred, King of Kent, imposed fines on anyone making an offering to demons.

In 697, the Ecclesiastical Council of Berkhamsted drove sorcerers out of the Church or had them fined.

In 750, the Archbishop of York forbade sacrifices to demons, vows at wells, stones, or trees, and the gathering of herbs while reciting incantations not of a Christian nature.

In the late nineteenth century, King Edward of Wessex and King Guthram of East Anglia passed laws against witches and diviners which were as severe as the laws against murderers and perjurers.

Also in the ninth century, King Alfred reiterated the Biblical statement that witches and wizards must not be suffered to live.

In 906, a work known as the *Canon Episcopi* castigated women who were "won over by the devil because of too vivid an imagination."

During the reign of Athelstan, son of Edward, from 925 to 940, the law held that murder by witchcraft was equal to ordinary homicide. In this period, priests were punished for saying masses over wax images as a means of placing a curse on someone.

In 959, King Edgar forbade worship at wells, casting spells, and practices involving elder trees and stones.

In 1008, King Ethelred forbade the practice of magic.

During the eleventh century, King Canute prohibited worship of heathen gods, the sun, the moon, wells, stones, or trees. The well-known incident in which the Danish king commanded the tide to retreat was meant to show the people that Canute was not a god and therefore had no control over the tide.

Until the end of the twelfth century, it was a common practice to throw accused witches, as well as criminals and adulterers, into deep water as a trial. Sometimes the right thumb of the accused was bound to the left large toe. If the accused sank, he was innocent; if he floated or swam, he was guilty. This practice was abolished in England in 1219 because the clergy discovered that it was derived from the Swedish pagan rite of sacrifice to the river gods.

In 1209, the Inquisition, begun by Pope Innocent III, launched its campaign against heresy, the effects of which were felt through the next five centuries. The first woman to be burned as a witch was Angèle, Lady of Labarthe, who was executed in Languedoc in 1275.

The Beginnings of the Inquisition

The intense and cruel persecution of witches known as the Inquisition was begun as a crusade against the Albigenses, members of a dualist sect which originated in the Languedoc region of France around 1140. The Albigenses, also known as Cathars, believed in good and evil as two opposing but equal powers which dominated the world. Although they accepted Christ as a saviour, they rejected the Catholic teachings concerning the physical resurrection of Christ and the forthcoming rebirth of faithful souls on Judgement Day. Their heretical idea of equating the forces of God with the evil forces of the Devil seemed to suggest that a person might choose to ally himself with the powers of the Devil. Witches, who became known as agents of the Devil, seemed to the Inquisitors to exemplify this kind of heresy.

The Black Mass and other rites which parodied the Church, probably arose as a form of rebellion against this relentless persecution. Persons accused of witchcraft were tortured excruciatingly until they confessed to meetings with the Devil, flights through the air to orgiastic Sabbat rituals, and possession of animal familiars. The present concept of early black witchcraft is derived largely from the descriptions given in the confessions of accused witches.

The Principles of the Inquisition

The guiding principles of the Inquisition were set forth in a work known as *Malleus Maleficarum* or *Hammer of Witches,* written in 1486 by Heinrich Kramer and Jakob Sprenger, the chief Inquisitors of Germany. This volume increased the fervor of the Inquisition by describing evil acts attributed to witches and by indicating the manner in which the witches should be handled. Some of the ideas expressed in the *Hammer* were:

1. Witches were responsible for the destruction of human life, cattle, and crops.
2. Witches could change themselves into animals.
3. Witches could fly.
4. Witches worked so secretly that they could only be brought to justice by a confession under torture.
5. Witches must be burned to death to prevent their spirits from returning.
6. No suspect must ever be released after torture.
7. The persecution must encompass folk superstition, which was also heretical, as well as actual witchcraft.
8. It is heretical to deny the existence of witchcraft or the Devil.

Other Inquisitors wrote treatises on witchcraft and demons. In France, Henry Boguet's *Discours Execrable des Sorciers* (1603) gave instructions on how to try those persons accused of sorcery. Martin Del Rio, a feared inquisitor of Flanders, wrote a similar book in 1611. King James I of England, a merciless persecutor of heretics, wrote a dialogue between two men called Philomathus and Epistemon. The latter expounded the king's own views and condemned sorcerers and diviners in a cold-blooded manner. French philosopher Jean Bodin, whose other works were of a more humane nature, also produced a book on the subject. His *La Dèmonomanie des Sorciers* (1582) was as harsh in its judgments as those of the Inquisitors.

These books included rules to be followed in examining and judging those who were brought to trial. Most were unethical by today's standards; all showed the inhumanity which was characteristic of the witch trials. Some of the rules taken from the various documents were:

1. Little children should be made to testify against their mothers.
2. Witches must be questioned and examined without warning, before they have time to confer with the Devil.
3. The examiner must look directly into the witch's eyes, for a witch cannot look squarely upon a man's face.

4. In order to wring a confession from the accused, the judge should at first pretend to be sympathetic with her plight of being misled by the Devil.
5. A witch must not be imprisoned alone, for she might confer with the Devil privately.
6. During the questioning, someone should be stationed in an adjoining room pretending to cry out under torture. This was meant to intimidate the witch.
7. A crafty spy should be placed among the prisoners in case the witch should confess in her cell.
8. A witch should be told that her comrades have betrayed and accused her, even if this is not the case.
9. If an old woman who is generally mistrusted touches a well person and he dies soon after, this is proof that the woman is a witch.
10. If a person is able to enter or leave a house whose doors and windows are closed, that person is a witch.
11. If three persons declare a woman to be a witch, she will be sentenced to death.
12. If one reputable man accuses someone of witchcraft, that person must be tortured until a confession is obtained.
13. The testimony of a condemned or infamous person is upheld in a witch trial.
14. A perjured person is worthy to testify against a witch.
15. It is known that a witch can cry no more than three tears. The Inquisitor must be certain that the accused does not substitute false tears.

The Examination and Torture

To bring a person to the Inquisitors, secret witnesses would report the suspicious behavior of the accused. This behavior included stirring a cauldron, chanting a healing spell, or even being distantly related to someone who had been convicted as a witch. The possession of magical equipment, such as wands, talismans, grimoires (books of magical instruction), or the sword used to draw magic circles, was sufficient evidence to send a person to the torture chamber.

The suspect was usually arrested at night, flung into a dark dungeon, and kept entirely isolated when not being questioned. Before the questioning, he was stripped and shaved to prevent his concealing any protective amulet which might save him.

A more humiliating and terrifying procedure was the search for the witch's mark, supposedly made by the Devil. Since this mark was reputedly insensitive to pain, a knife-like instrument known as a "witch-pricker" was thrust into parts of the body to find the mark. Any wart or mole found on the body was assumed to be the witch mark.

Persons accused of witchcraft were often subjected to tests known as "ordeals." The water ordeal mentioned earlier was one. Another ordeal required the accused to be weighed against a large copy of the Bible. If she outweighed the Bible, she was innocent. At the height of the Inquisition's frenzy, however, innocence proven by such a simple test was easily disregarded.

One characteristic attributed to witches was the inability to read a prayer or passage from the Bible correctly. Therefore, the reading of religious material served as a test for accused witches. *The History of Witches and Wizards* (c. 1700) describes a case in which the accused was asked to recite the Lord's Prayer. She was able to say the words correctly until she reached the phrase "And lead us not into temptation." No matter how often she attempted to correct herself, the words came out as either "And lead us into temptation" or "And lead us not into no temptation." It is not difficult to imagine how a poor and illiterate old woman, brought to the point of hysteria, might find herself repeatedly stumbling on the familiar words, thus proving her guilt.

All questioning was accompanied by torture. The object was to make the prisoner confess not only his own guilt, but that of several friends and neighbors.

During the early part of the questioning, the "preliminary" tortures were used. These included a few turns of the thumbscrews or a relatively mild session on the rack, an instrument which stretched a person from both ends

The main tortures used by the Inquisition were known as *strappado* and *squassation.* In strappado, the accused was suspended from the ceiling by a rope, with weights attached to his feet. Squassation was the same except that the rope from which the prisoner was suspended would be suddenly released, then tightened.

Other tortures included tearing of flesh with red-hot pincers, severing of limbs, immersing in scalding lime, and scrubbing with wire brushes. During the tortures, a notary would take down every word uttered by the accused so that a confession might be made from his anguished mutterings.

Those who confessed under torture were granted the mercy of being strangled before they were burned. Those who withdrew their confessions were burned alive as relapsed heretics. When prisoners died during torture, the Inquisitors would say that Satan himself had caused their deaths to prevent these witches from revealing his secrets.

Joan of Arc

Joan of Arc, the celebrated Maid of Orleans, was among those tried by the Inquisition. The basis of the accusation against her was her declaration that disembodied voices had guided her in fulfilling her mission. The Inquisition wished to determine whether these voices were of a divine or diabolic origin.

The girl was captured by the English at the Siege of Orleans and brought to the Inquisitors. She was publicly exhibited in a cramped cage as an example of a witch.

During her trial, she answered the questions well, but later made a confession. Desiring to charge her as a heretic as well as a witch, Inquisition officials tricked her into wearing men's clothing, which was considered a heretical act. Angered by this plot, she retracted her confession, enabling the Inquisitors to order her burned alive as a relapsed heretic.

By a strange twist of fate, two of the men who had caused her death came to miserable ends themselves. The bishop who had originally condemned her died suddenly a few years after her death. His body was thrown into the common sewer. Charles VII, who had abandoned her, starved to death slowly and painfully out of fear of being poisoned by his son.

The Mania in the Convents

A series of witch trials occured in seventeenth-century France which involved several handsome and charismatic priests who were accused of bewitching the nuns of their convents. The most famous of these incidents was described in a book by Aldous Huxley entitled *Devils of Loudon* and later made into a movie called *The Devils*. The Devils of Loudon manifested themselves in an Ursuline convent of that town, whose priest-confessor was the suave Père Urbain Grandier. Led by the Mother Superior, the entire convent of nuns became seized by fits and began to blaspheme in strange voices. Cardinal Richelieu, who had been antagonized by Father Grandier, found the means to make a case against the priest for bewitching the nuns. Several accounts indicate that he may have been guilty of seducing the nuns, who then became hysterical from fear and guilt.

A very damaging piece of evidence against Grandier was a pact made with the Devil. In this pact, the priest promised to serve and worship the Devil. The actual pact, signed by Urban Grandier in his blood, is in the Bibliothèque Nationale in France.

Grandier was arrested and tortured, then burned alive. His ghost was known to haunt the town of Loudon and those who destroyed him.

A similar case occurred at a convent in Provence, where a priest named Père Louis Gauffridi had seduced a young girl who had been entrusted to him. He made her believe that he had taken her to a witches' Sabbat and gave her a silver ring engraved with cabbalistic symbols as a token of their marriage in the sight of the Devil.

Bewildered by these strange occurrences, the girl became mad and the whole convent followed suit. Another nun denounced the priest as a witch, and he was burned at the stake in Aix.

Still another convent, this time at Louviers, was upset by a girl who had been seduced by a priest. The residents of the convent became involved in orgies and lesbianism, and the girl denounced several of the other nuns as witches. Most of them were hanged, but there is no record of the girl's conviction or death.

The Witchcraft Cover-up

In 1673, several French priests told authorities that they had heard in the confessional of a group of poisoners in Paris who had been commissioned on several occasions by women who wanted to be rid of their husbands. No evidence was found at the time, but four years later, police raided the home of a fortune-teller and uncovered a ring of fortune-tellers who were also performing abortions and poisonings. Wax figures were found which had been used for witchcraft, and the rooms contained evidence of a Black Mass and the sacrifice of newborn babies to Satan.

Since several of the witches proved to be noblemen and included Madame Montespan, mistress of King Louis XIV, the king covered up the episode and most of the noblemen escaped punishment. Some of the less wealthy fortune-tellers were tortured and burned alive, including a colorful personality known as La Voisin.

The Death of Bluebeard

The original Bluebeard, whose reputation has caught the imagination of storytellers, was a French nobleman named Gilles de Rais. This notorious gentleman turned to alchemy and sorcery in order to increase his wealth. Perhaps bored by the wealth he attained, he began torturing and killing children for sexual gratification. Over the years, he also murdered six of his seven wives. Eventually, he confessed and was strangled and burned at Nantes in 1440.

Witch Trials in England

Most of the witches persecuted in England were old and extremely poor. The witch hunts in that country were led by the Puritans and extreme Protestants in the sixteenth and seventeenth centuries. Henry VIII and his daughter Elizabeth I were particularly vindictive against witches.

The most famous trials in England were those of the witches of Northamptonshire and Lancashire, and of

Elizabeth Sawyer, known as the Witch of Edmonton. Her trial was typical of those held in England. She was asked the details of her first acquaintance with the Devil, to which she answered that he entered her while she was blaspheming and cursing. Her testimony related that the Devil then agreed to serve her in injuring her enemies if she would worship him, give him her soul and body, and nourish him with her blood. This confession naturally led to conviction and death.

The Inquisition in Other Countries of Europe

Although the Inquisition spread beyond England and France, it was not felt as heavily in the other European countries. Other than in Scotland, and for less than a decade in Germany, only isolated incidents of persecution were noted in such countries as Sweden, Ireland, and the Netherlands.

The worst period of persecution in Germany was from 1623 to 1632, when Bamberg was ruled by the prince-bishop Godfried Johann Georg, a cruel witch-hater. Bishops were allowed to confiscate the property of those who were condemned, which added to their zeal in uncovering witches.

In 1669 in Sweden, children of the town of Mora claimed to have been lured by women to a Sabbat held in a meadow called Blocula. There the women were said to have made a pact with the Devil. Seventy women and fifty children were found guilty in this incident.

In Ireland in 1324, a woman called Lady Kyteler was accused of sacrificing live cockerels to Satan, repudiating the Catholic Church, and having a familiar in the shape of a black, shaggy dog.

In Scotland, James VI, who later became James I of England, particularly attacked white witches, whom he considered to be most dangerous.

The most famous Scottish witch, Isobel Gowdie, gives us a picture of Scottish witchcraft in her confession. According to her testimony, the witches met in covens of thirteen, each with an animal familiar. They would begin the Sabbat by raising the wind in the name of the Devil. The Devil would give each witch an elf-arrow to shoot, in his name. Instead of a bow, the witches' thumbs were used to propel the arrows.

The witches could go out in the shape of a hare, cat, or crow, and could turn others into these shapes as well. When leaving for the Sabbat, each woman put a broom into her bed which changed into the shape of a woman in order to fool her husband into thinking that she was there.

In the Netherlands, the persecution was somewhat less severe because of a writer named Jean Weir, who attempted in his works to convince the Inquisition that many persons accused as witches were merely eccentric or mentally unbalanced.

The Persecution of Witches in the United States

The witch hunts of the United States were limited to a few states. Aside from the extensive persecution in Massachusetts, there were no more than one or two instances in each state.

In 1790, in Cahokie, Illinois, an African slave was hanged for murdering his master by witchcraft and another slave was shot for this crime. In the same area, an old woman was suspected of destroying persons and property with incantations.

In Princess Anne County, Virginia, a quiet woman named Grace Sherwood was accused of witchcraft in 1706. Her accusers claimed that she had sailed across the Atlantic in an eggshell, as gypsy witches were said to do, and brought back strange herbs for spells. There is no record of her conviction on this evidence.

When William Penn was justice of the peace in Pennsylvania, he tried two Swedish women who were indicted as witches. Because of a flaw in the procedure, however, they were released.

In 1712, some persons in South Carolina were accused of witchcraft and were condemned to be burned. They were burned slightly but not fatally, and they brought suit in court for damages, but were not remunerated.

In 1646, the first witch to be executed in New England

died in Hartford, Connecticut.

Massachusetts, the setting for the notorious witch hunt of Salem Village, was the home of Cotton Mather, the minister who became known for his investigation of witches and his writing on the subject.

Reverend Mather became interested in a family named Goodwin, whose children were all bewitched except for the eldest boy, who was grown, and the youngest, an infant. The afflicted children would act like cats, geese, dogs, and birds. They would suddenly and unaccountably be striken deaf, dumb, or blind.

Cotton Mather took the eldest girl to live in his home in order to study the case more closely. The girl would contort her features, fly and dive, and ride around on an invisible horse. She was impudent to the minister and often interrupted his work. A local woman was accused by the child as the witch who tormented her. With concentrated prayer, the girl's condition gradually improved.

In 1692, the events occurred which led up to the trials and deaths of many residents of Salem Village and the surrounding area. The trouble started in the home of the local minister, the Reverend Samuel Parris. His West Indian servant had amused the minister's young daughter and niece with ghost stories and soon the young girls of the neighborhood gathered around the servant to watch her practice necromancy and divination.

Possibly tortured by guilt over these forbidden pastimes, some of the girls became hysterical and soon all of them were exhibiting strange symptoms. The slave, Tituba, was accused as a witch and brought to trial, where she named two other local women, Sarah Good and Sarah Osbourne as accomplices. Before long, one name after another was added to the list of the accused. The girls accused Martha Corey, an upright woman with a tendency to criticize, and her husband, who was tortured to death instead of hanged. A seven-year-old girl was accused, as well as a respected man and his pregnant wife. A long list of respectable citizens were condemned and many were hanged before the girls lost their credibility by accusing a member of Cotton Mather's family and the wife of a prominent minister of another town. After September 22, 1692, no one was hanged and in April of 1693, the remaining suspects were freed. In 1711, there was a reversal of the verdicts in some cases and compensation was made to the heirs of those unjustly accused.

Later Persecution and Legislation

By the early eighteenth century, the Inquisition had virtually died and legislation, particularly in England, began to reflect a waning of the intense hatred of witches. As recently as the twentieth century, attacks were made on persons believed to be witches, but these were isolated cases, often in remote areas.

In 1894, in Clonmel, Ireland, a man thought that his wife was a fairy and burned her in the presence of thirteen people. All were found guilty of manslaughter.

In 1836, in Danzig, an old woman was thrown into the sea. Because she did not sink, she was beaten to death with sticks and stones.

In 1927, a German sorcerer told a farmer that his wife had bewitched his cattle. The farmer beat her for two weeks until she died.

In 1928, a Pennsylvania "witch doctor," or white witch, accused a man of being a witch and asked him to surrender a lock of his hair to use as a counter-spell. He refused and was murdered by his neighbors.

In 1736, capital punishment was abolished in cases of witchcraft in England.

In 1746, what was probably the last burning for witchcraft in the civilized world occurred in Guavina, Peru.

In 1822, George IV declared that "All persons pretending to be Gipsies, all persons pretending to tell Fortunes, or using any Subtle Craft, Means, or Device, By Palmistry or otherwise to deceive or impose upon any of His Majesty's subjects shall be adjudged 'Common Rogues and Vagabonds' and sentenced as such."

As England removed its laws against witchcraft, other countries followed suit, and the fear of witchcraft was diminished throughout the western world.

3. Contemporary Witches

WITCHES WERE "LIBERATED" in England by the Fraudulent Mediums Act of 1951, which by condemning mediums rather than witches, made witchcraft an entirely legal activity. The new witchcraft which arose was evidently influenced by the writings of Margaret Murray, whose theory of the continuity of witchcraft has been strongly disputed, and by Aleister Crowley, who introduced the principle of gaining power by submerging the ego.

Black, White, and Gray Witches

The witches of the Inquisition, who parodied Christianity, made human sacrifices, and placed curses on their enemies, were black witches. Today, black witches are likely to be known as satanists, and those comparatively few covens of black witches have gone far underground. Here and there, an individual dabbling in the occult has attempted to work black magic; many have been shaken by the experience.

The majority of witches belonging to organized covens, or witches groups, are white witches. Their goal is to use their powers to heal and help others and to maintain a feeling of spiritual and emotional well-being through "covening."

The covens are tightly knit groups, usually of thirteen members. The leader is the High Priestess, who is assisted by the High Priest. Witches are truly liberated woman, for their chief deity is the Earth Goddess, who is represented on earth by the High Priestess. The Horned God, represented by the High Priest, is revered, but with slightly less awe than is accorded the Goddess.

The deputy of the High Priestess is known as the Maiden,

and the remaining members are covenites. Each member of a coven uses a special name by which he is known to others in the coven.

The place in which the coven meets is known as the *covenstead.* Most covens prohibit group sex or the use of drugs. Some covens perform their rites in the nude to symbolize the casting off of material possessions, but the traditional witches, who follow certain Druidic practices, prefer to wear long, flowing robes. Witches usually choose to keep their hair long, not only because they believe that is more natural, but because long hair can more easily feel the movement of the winds. Their feet are bare outdoors in order to maintain contact with the earth.

Contrary to popular belief, a male witch is not called a warlock; he is simply a male witch. A warlock is a magician or sorcerer who performs complex rituals in order to achieve certain goals.

White witches often end a speech or piece of writing with the ancient phrase, "So mote it be."

Besides the covens, Pagan Groups exist, which are composed of those who believe in the Earth Goddess and other principles of witchcraft, but are not initiated as witches. This type of group is not as structured as a coven and may be extended to include as many members as is practical. Both covens and Pagan Groups emphasize the need for individual members to free themselves of friction with other members in order to relate as effectively as possible within the group. One covenite referred to the interaction in his group as "unstructured group therapy."

In addition to the black and white witches, there are a handful of gray witches who, as the name implies, are not totally committed to either extreme. Like the white witches, they often use their magic to help others, although they are equally capable of cursing someone.

In *The Psychic World of California,* David St. Clair describes a curse by a gray witch named Barbara. After a visit to her family in the Midwest, she called out to her father from the steps of the airplane: "There will be rain for forty days and forty nights and your crops will be ruined." From that day, it rained for three solid weeks. Barbara's sister called the gray witch and asked her to lift the curse because their father's tomato plants were being destroyed.

The chief characteristic of gray witches is that they worship no specific deity. They believe in vaguely defined forces of good and evil, but not in God, Satan, or the Earth Goddess. They believe that their power comes from themselves rather than from an outside force. They avoid prayers and rituals and have no High Priestess or Priest.

Gray witches can conduct séances, investigate hauntings, exorcise poltergeists, and remove hexes. They also practice candle power, which makes use of different color candles to achieve various aims.

Wicca

The religion of Wicca is practiced by white witches, as well as by persons who claim that they are not actually witches.

Wicca was founded in England by Dr. Gerald Gardner, who claimed that this religion existed in prehistoric times and has been handed down in some families through the generations. Gardner was the first High Priest of Wicca, and was successful in establishing witchcraft in the British Isles. To upgrade the image of witches, he made several appearances on television and established a museum of witchcraft on the Isle of Man.

Wicca is a religion that worships nature. The emphasis on herb lore and the supremacy of the Earth Goddess are essential Wiccan beliefs. The witches' calendar reflects the natural turning points of the year—the solstices, the waxing and waning of the moon, and the changing of the seasons. Four annual festivals are held: Candlemas, on February Eve, Beltane, on May Eve, Lammas on August 1, and Halloween, on October 31.

Wicca is not entirely standardized in its practices and ceremonies. There is some variation from one coven to another, and it is therefore difficult to determine which rituals are truly a part of Wicca and which are practiced by a particular coven.

At important ceremonies and meetings, a prayer is read from *The Book of Shadows,* the Wicca handbook. This book also lists the degrees of attainment in Wicca craft and the way in which they may be achieved.

An important goal of Wicca is to reach fulfillment through the eight paths: trance, meditation, binding with cords, flagellation, wine, dancing, and spells. The eighth path, called the Great Rite, is the sexual act, sometimes performed symbolically. This act is the culmination of many important ceremonies for it is supposed to release the life force in the universe.

Wicca Ceremonies

The witches' business meeting is known as the *Estabat,* or *Esbat.* The purpose of these meetings is to help individuals by concentrating the combined psychic power of the coven on a particular problem.

The first step, as in any Wicca ceremony, is the drawing of the magic circle. The High Priestess must redraw the circle with her sword before each meeting to properly enclose and protect the powers.

Inside the circle, the High Priestess stands alone in silent psychic communion with the Goddess, who is represented by a statue. After a prayer is read from *The Book of Shadows,* the entire coven begins chanting and rhythmic dancing. This activity is meant to build up a concentration of energy, which is referred to as a "cone of power." This power is directed toward the individual whom the coven is trying to help.

Refreshments of cake and wine are traditionally served.

The initiation of a postulant into a coven is an important ceremony and is performed only on one of the four annual festival days. Covens do not seek converts and have high standards for accepting new members. Usually a potential witch must undergo a training period of a year and a day before being initiated. A witch whose powers are hereditary may not require initiation, as it is assumed that he will have the proper understanding and knowledge of the craft.

Specific initiation ceremonies vary from one coven to another, but there are certain basic rituals. Initiation takes place within the magic circle. Sometimes the postulant must have a ritual bath before the ceremony in order to be cleansed of former ways. In many covens, the postulant is naked, blindfolded, and bound with cords during the ceremony. The High Priestess reads a passage which begins:

> Listen to the words of the Great Mother who was of old also called among men Artimis : Astarte : Dione : Melusine : Aphrodite : Ceridwen : Dana : Arianrod : Bride : and by many other names.

The reading ends:

> I who am the beauty of the green earth : and the white moon amongst the stars : and the mystery of the waters : and the desire of the heart of man : call unto thy soul : arise and come unto me.

Sometimes the coven sings a song called "Eko Eko Azarak":

> Darksome night and shining moon,
> East then south then west then north,
> Harken to the witches' rune
> Here I come to call thee forth.
>
> Earth and water, air and fire,
> Wand and pentacle and sword,
> Work ye now to my desire,
> Harken ye unto my word.
>
> Cords and censer, scourge and knife,
> Powers of the witches' blade.
> Waken all ye unto life,
> Come ye as the charm is made.
>
> Queen of heaven, queen of hell,
> Horned hunter of the night,
> Lend your power unto the spell,
> Work my will by magic rite.
>
> Power of land and sway of sea,
> Might of moon and gift of sun,
> Do as I will, and let it be,
> Chant the spell and it be done.
>
> Eko, Eko Azarak
> Eko, Eko Zamilak
> Eko, Eko Cernunnos
> Eko, Eko Aradia

The postulant is then questioned on his knowledge of witchcraft while a sword is held poised over his heart. After the questioning is finished, he says, "I have two perfect words, perfect love and perfect trust."

The High Priestess answers, "All who have are doubly welcome. I give you a third to pass through this dread door." She kisses the postulant and announces to the witch gods that he is ready to join the craft. As she moves three times around the circle, the other witches kneel.

The High Priest stands outstretched at the altar, gives his secret name, and recites a proclamation in Runic. The new member is given five kisses and a new witch-name. Sometimes there is more chanting and the Great Rite is performed. The new witch promises to honor and keep the secrets of the craft. He rises, is consecrated with oil and wine, and is unbound. The High Priest presents him with the tools of the craft: the magic sword, the athame knife, a white-handled knife, the wand, the pentacle, and incense. He receives the ritual scourge for purification, is proclaimed a witch, and the circle is closed.

A Wicca wedding is a special and solemn ceremony. A special area is consecrated by the High Priest for the magic circle to be drawn. Sometimes the priest wears a crown of pentacles; in some parts of the ceremony the couple wear these crowns. The High Priest and Priestess may wear white robes and the couple often wears brightly colored robes of a loosely woven material.

The wedding text, known as the "handfasting ceremony," is read from *The Book of Shadows*. In some covens, the High Priest makes symbolic love to the High Priestess by kissing the length of her body. She then calls down a cone of power on the circle.

The bride and groom jump over a broomstick to guarantee fertility. Their blood is mixed from small cuts made on the arms and hands to symbolize a complete physical and spiritual union.

The priest addresses the couple; then there is sometimes dancing.

A witch couple vows to remain married only "as long as love shall last," but a high percentage of witches remain married for a lifetime. Even if divorce occurs, both partners continue to maintain the responsibility for the care of their children.

Modern Covens and Societies

It has been estimated that there are several thousand white witches in many of the large cities of the United States. The figure given for Chicago is six thousand. This would mean that there are several hundred covens in some cities. Most smaller cities and towns have at least a few covens. Many witches prefer to live in a rural area which brings them closer to nature. Each coven attracts a different type of membership.

One Chicago coven is led by High Priestess Mary L. This coven consists of eight men and women, three of whom hold doctoral degrees. The other five are in various professional or executive positions.

Mary herself is a psychiatric social worker. She combines her two lifestyles in her work by treating some patients with psychotherapy and some with magic, according to their needs. In difficult cases, the whole coven works together on the treatment by concentrating on a lock of hair or a photograph of the patient.

Many mild disorders have been cured by the coven, and fifteen young men have been kept from the draft by its collective powers.

An important coven in Manhattan is the New York coven of Welsh Traditionalist Witches. The coven is headed by High Priestess Kay Smith, known as Lady Viviane, and High Priest Ed Buczynski, whose witch-name is Hermes. According to an article in *Witchcraft Digest*, in which the two witches discuss the role of the High Priest and Priestess in the coven, the leaders of the coven share the combined roles of husband and wife, sister and brother, soul-mate lovers, and parents of the covenites. As the moon waxes and wanes, the role of the High Priestess changes subtly to express the three aspects of the Goddess—maiden, mother, and crone, or Wise Woman. Her relationship to the High Priest changes as she assumes each of these roles. While the High Priest and Priestess share a strong bond of psychic love, they are usually not involved in a sexual or emotional relationship and each is often married to someone else.

The Delphian coven at Lander, Wyoming, lives even more closely to the land than most witches. Under the leadership of the High Priestess Bonnie Sherlock, the coven practices its rites in a breathtakingly beautiful setting.

This coven has a close bond with the American Indians and borrows from their lore. Their charms and talismans are made from beads, horn, feathers, and animal hair. Like the Indians, these witches communicate with nature spirits in sacred places.

Using their hands to create the things which they need is a part of the coven's lifestyle. Sabbat wines are made within the coven. The witches make their own candles and their loosely flowing robes.

The Delphian Priestess does not believe in nude rituals, for she feels that nakedness is a symbol of subjugation and that it is more aesthetically pleasing to see a coven dressed in brightly colored robes.

Sometimes there is rivalry between witches of different covens. In *Patterns of Prophecy*, Alan Vaughan describes an experience which happened to a friend, Justine Glass, an author of books on witchcraft, who joined a coven in 1968. The leader of another coven asked her to co-author a book with him, but she refused. The rival witch claimed to have put a curse on her, but it evidently backfired and he committed suicide within a few months. During that same year, Ms. Glass, who had previously been in excellent health, died of a painful liver ailment.

In addition to the covens, witches' societies exist in the United States for the benefit of all covens and persons seeking to become witches.

A major craft organization is WICA, which stands for Witches International Craft Association. The purpose of WICA, according to Dr. Leo Louis Martello, who edits the WICA newsletter, is to gain religious freedom and civil rights and to upgrade the image of witches by dispelling myths and prejudices.

The WEB, or Witches' Encounter Bureau, is available to anyone who is in need of a "contact." This refers to persons seeking to meet other witches or to apply for membership in a coven. Although covens do not recruit members, they desire to remain available to those who are sincere in their wish to join the craft.

Personalities in the World of Witchcraft

As in any other field, witchcraft has its share of outstanding personalities which range from the sophisticated image of the "official witch of Los Angeles" to the strange and sinister figure of Aleister Crowley. Each of these witches and wizards, by gaining public recognition, has contributed in some way to the current concept of witchcraft.

One of the well-known contemporary witches is the British witch Sybil Leek. With her strong features, full figure, and long loose dresses, she resembles the Earth Mother worshiped by the white witches. Although she has been labeled as a white witch herself, Ms. Leek claims that this is a modern term applied by self-styled witches.

Having grown up in the craft, she can consider herself a hereditary witch with a lineage that dates back to the Stone Age. She admits to having been involved in black magic, but she has given it up to devote her time to astrology and writing. As a successful astrologer and businesswoman, Ms. Leek has, in addition to her numerous published books, an astrology magazine and other astrology-related business ventures.

In 1970, a young man named Isaac Bonewitz became the first person to graduate from an American university with a bachelor's degree in Arts and Magic. To obtain this unusual degree, he persuaded the administration of the University of California at Berkely to allow him to pursue a specific series of courses which would make him competent in the subject. Among the topics which he studied were astrology, Tarot cards, hypnosis, the Cabbala, and medieval witchcraft.

During his undergraduate years, he was known to his fellow students as "the Wizard of Mod." They would come to him for love potions, hexes, and cures which he dispensed willingly. Bonewitz plans eventually to obtain a Ph.D. in magic.

Two witches who would probably be considered "nonwitches" by many members of the craft are the "official witch of New York City" and the "official witch of Los Angeles."

The former was an ex-chorus girl known as Witch Hazel,

who was given her title in order to conduct a "witch-in" in Central Park. Her chief function was invoking love spells.

Louise Huebner, the official witch of Los Angeles, received her title for a festival in the Hollywood Bowl and refused to relinquish it afterward. The title became an asset on which she could capitalize to aid the sale of her books and her recording of chants. Although Ms. Huebner claims genuine magical powers inherited through six generations, she believes that it is unnecessary to use her magic to help others.

A discussion of modern witchcraft would not be complete without a glimpse of Aleister Crowley, whose writings influenced the leaders of the new witchcraft.

At the age of twelve, Crowley crucified a toad as an experiment in the invocation of occult powers. He then began calling down curses on those who offended him.

One of those who received the curse of Aleister Crowley was the High Priest of the Order of the Golden Dawn, an intellectual secret society. Crowley wished to become the leader himself, and in order to achieve this end, he was said to have called up an army of forty-nine demons headed by Beelzebub to destroy the current High Priest. The man died, but instead of becoming the new leader, Crowley was expelled from the group.

Crowley then assumed leadership of a German occult group known as OTO, Orders of the Templars of the Orient. His followers were required to slash themselves with a razor each time they said "I." This discipline was intended to eliminate all sense of self. The putting aside of self is one of the principles of modern magic, but is not usually learned in such a gory manner.

Crowley authored poetry and prose of a sinister and sexually powerful mood. He would sign himself "The Beast," which suited the diabolic appearance of his later years. In spite of his emphasis on control, his own life was filled with moral weakness. He was a heroin addict for many years and he fathered several illegitimate children.

In 1920, he established the notorious Abbey of Thelema in Sicily, but was expelled from Italy three years later. His last words before he died were, "I am perplexed."

Every religion or cult has its detractors, and Wicca is no

exception. One of these is Owen Rachleff, who teaches courses in the occult at New York University's Department of Continuing Education. Mr. Rachleff frankly admits to being a "debunker of the occult." His recent book, *The Occult Conceit*, has brought the wrath of white witches upon him.

Exception is taken particularly to his statement: "Why, when they could find love, peace, and strength in any of the established religions or even those of the more unorthodox variety, have they chosen the ancient cult of witchcraft?"

The question can be answered wisely only by a member of the craft, and judging by the number of white witches in this country, there are many members of the Earth Religion who could answer that question at least to their own satisfaction.

4. The Devil

THE DEVIL was a prominent figure in the heyday of black witchcraft. Witches made pacts with him, worshiped him, and joined him at the Sabbat. Satan has always had his followers among non-witches as well.

The Bible contains references to Satan and his legions of demons which show how the concepts of the devils differ in the Old and New Testament. The Hebrew word for Satan means "adversary," which expresses the Old Testament concept of Satan as a being who persisted in recognizing beliefs which were false.

With the advent of Christianity and the New Testament, the concept of the Devil as a deceiver who leads men into temptation began. Revelation 14:9 describes the fall of Satan from heaven: "And the great dragon was thrown down, that ancient serpent, who is called the Devil and Satan, the deceiver of the whole world."

As Christianity spread across Europe, the Church became greatly concerned with the Devil. The efforts to frighten people by dramatizing the powers of Satan paradoxically caused certain groups to be attracted to the being who promised pleasure, however temporary, while Christianity was asking them to deny themselves.

An early belief which led to Satan worship was the idea that the world is predominantly evil and therefore must be guided by an evil power. Since Satan was the prime source of evil, a logical culmination of this belief was the acceptance of Satan as a god. His worshipers attempted to invert religious practices by repudiating the Commandments, desecrating churches, defiling altars, perverting sexual practices, and celebrating a Black Mass.

The Black Mass, originally known as the Mass of St. Secaire, was first celebrated in the Basque region of France.

The purpose of the early ceremony was not only to honor Satan, but to bring death upon an enemy. The ritual was usually held in a ruined church and conducted by an ordained priest. A Black Host was consecrated and "unholy water," in which an unbaptized baby was drowned, was used instead of sacramental wine.

The Demonic Hierarchy

Satanists and others who study the nature of the underworld have found references throughout the Bible and other early literature to demons other than the Devil, who is sometimes called Satan or Lucifer. The wide range of these references indicates the presence of a vast demonic hierarchy consisting of many legions of demons, each performing a specific function under the direction of Satan.

The Reverend Terry Taylor, priest of a contemporary Satanic cult in Chicago lists eighty members of the hierarchy. Other sources list some of the names with slight changes of spelling. Each of these demons has legions of lesser demons under him.

Altogether, there are said to be about seven million demons in the world, although some sources give a figure as high as 1,758,064,176. The ancient formula for figuring the number of demons requires multiplying the Great Pythagorean Number (1234321) by six. The answer is 7,405,926, which is a substantial number of demons.

The highest-ranking demon is, of course, Satan himself, known as the emperor of the Grand Grimoire. His demon prince is Beelzebub, also known as Lord of the Flies. The grand duke, Astaroth, counsels and directs fallen angels.

The Commander-in-Chief, Put Satanachia, has power over mothers. He has knowledge of all the planets and can provide animal familiars for human witches. Satan's commander, Agliarept, controls Europe and Asia Minor. He also controls the past and future and is responsible for creating enmity among men.

Beelzebub's lieutenant-general is called Fleurety. He controls Africa and is skilled in the use of poisonous and hallucinatory herbs. He works his evil by night, in the company of his large group of familiars, putting lust in men's minds and causing war.

Sargatanas is Astaroth's brigadier-major. He can make humans lose their memory and transport them to another part of the world. He is capable of invading the secret lives of humans, creeping into their most private thoughts.

Nebiros is Astaroth's field marshall. He controls North America and is capable of using animals to carry out his vicious schemes.

The prime minister is known as Lucifuge Rofocale. He controls wealth and worldly goods, inflicts disease and deformities, causes earthquakes, and destroys religious deities.

Each of the remaining seventy-two demons has a particular function to perform in bringing evil to the world. A few of these demons perform a neutral or occasionally a beneficent function.

The seers are Vassago, Amon, Barbatos, Gusion, Botis, Purson, Berith, and Caim, who see the future, and Raum, who uses his vision to divine acts of theft.

Baal and Balam are able to cause men or animals to become invisible.

Beleth, Saleos, Vual, and Gomory are able to incite lust in a man. Eligor causes war as well as lust, while Sytry is concerned with nudity.

The demons who bring war are Lerajie, Allocen, Cimeries, and Furcas, who is also a teacher. Other demon teachers are Vapula, who teaches the sciences, Solas, who teaches astronomy, and Naberius, who teaches both science and astrology.

Several demons have power over the elements and forces of nature. Agares causes earthquakes. Furfur controls thunder, lightening, and strong winds. Vine can demolish great wall barriers and cause storms at sea. Procel can affect the temperature of any water, and can make it extremely hot or cold. The demon Seera can control time, so that it will appear to pass more rapidly or more slowly.

The ability to harm man's physical body is important to demons. Andras and Flauros are the killers. Markas causes diseases, while Shax can destroy sight and hearing. Abduscius crushes men with uprooted trees, and Sabnack decays and torments a man's body. Halpus causes destruction by fire and water. Aini also destroys by fire, while Glasyalubolas incites men to kill one another.

Three demons have power over the dead. Murmur controls the soul of the deceased. Bifrons and Bune change bodies to another burial place. Bifrons also lights candles on the graves.

The demons who control drugs and poisons are aeuathin, Morax, and Foras. Bathin is also responsible for the disappearance of men and cities.

Another group of demons can enter the minds and souls of men. Dantalian can change men's good thoughts to evil. Ipor creates false courage. Malpas destroys men's desires, and Paimon subjects men to his will. Gamygin influences the souls of sinners. Zepar can enter women's minds and drive them mad.

Ronobe, Forneus, and Phoenix confuse men's minds by speaking in tongues or parables.

Andrealphus can change men into birds, while Ose has the power to transform humans into any shape at all without their knowledge. Orias transforms men and can give titles as well. Gaap can transport men at will from one place to another.

Valefor influences theft and Andromatius causes disorder among thieves.

Exorcists should know about three particular demons. Focalor is capable of destroying the exorcist during his rites. Orabas and Marchosias, a strong demon, can be a protection to him. Other minor demons perform various duties:

> 1. Asmoday, also known as Asmodeus, guards the hidden treasure. 2. Amy is a trader of other spirits. 3. Zagan changes human blood into oil, then into water. 4. Vepar inflicts worms. 5. Valac will deliver serpents on command. 6. Decarabia produces birds or familiars. 7. Belial demands sacrifices.

Another demon, Behemoth, is mentioned in the Bible. He is known as a giant demon of great animal strength. Behemoth is usually depicted as an elephant with a large round stomach, standing upright.

Leviathan, the incubus, and Belphegor, who was worshiped by the Moabites, are also mentioned in the Old

Testament.

The incubus and succubus demons were two kinds of demons who would descend upon humans in the night for sexual perversions. In medieval times, the incubus was also thought to cause nightmares.

The New Testament also describes Abbadon or Apollyon, the Destroyer, one of the destroying angels of the Apocalypse.

The Arabs believe in three demons, Munkir, Neki, and Sachra El-marid.

Representations of the Devil

The Devil and the demons have always been a favorite subject of artists and engravers. The ideas of different countries on the role of the Devil are reflected in the changes in the way in which he is depicted.

The ancient cultures tended to attribute animal characteristics to both gods and demons. The Assyrians and the Babylonians depicted the Devil with the head of a lion and the feet of an eagle. The Egyptians represented the Devil sometimes as a baboon, sometimes as a wolf-like creature. Various medieval representations of the Devil show him as a dragon, he-goat, wolf, cat, owl, or half-human form.

In the fifteenth century, the great concern with the Devil which was propagated by the Inquisition gave rise to numerous illustrations. Dürer's *Apocalypse*, printed in Germany in 1498, shows Lucifer, the chief of the rebellious angels, and the battle in heaven between St. Michael and Satan. Jacobus de Teramo's *Das Buch Belial*, printed in 1493, illustrates the legend of King Solomon conjuring the demon Belial.

The Black Plague of the sixteenth century gave impetus to the Inquisition, which utilized the epidemic as an example of the work of devils and witches. The Demon of the Plague, causing sickness in men, was a popular illustration.

During the fourteenth through sixteenth centuries, the "morality posters" utilized depictions of demons to promote religious or political issues. These works showed various examples of behavior which was considered improper or immoral. In each case, a demon was shown inspiring the disfavored action or punishing those who were guilty of such conduct.

A fourteenth-century carved tablet showed English alewives being carried to hell for selling bad ale.

The Devil of Counterfeit was represented on a fifteenth century handbill attributed to Albrecht Dürer. Also by Dürer is a work depicting the Demon of Dice and the terrible fate of dice-players. This scene shows the Devil, with a goat's head, tempting the gamblers, who are shown in a subsequent illustration suffering terrible deaths.

Geoffrey de Latour Landry's *Ritter vom Turm*, printed in 1493, contains an illustration of demons making women gossip during Mass. Also in this work is an illustration entitled "The Demon of Vanity and the Coquette," which shows a girl looking in the mirror and seeing, instead of her face, the Devil's backside. The Devil is shown with a goat-like face.

The furor of the Reformation caused many handbills to be distributed by both sides, each claiming that the Devil was the leader of the opposing faction.

A fifteenth-century French Reform handbill depicts the "Papist Devil," a fiery creature decked in Papal attire, with the words "Ego Sum Papa," meaning "I am the Pope" over his head.

A sixteenth century German poster shows the Papist crowning the Devil's pig. The pig was often used as a symbol of Satan.

An anti-Lutheran pamphlet printed in Germany in 1518 depicts a Reform minister officiating at the marriage of a fool and a she-devil.

Seventeenth century pamphlets were used to denounce the Puritans or to warn against vices. For example, an anti-Puritan pamphlet of 1642 shows the Round-head as a devil.

Later pamphlets castigated the vices of smoking and usury. Thus, an English poster of 1618 warned against the devil of tobacco "drinking," while a seventeenth-century poster warning against loan sharks showed a devil formed out of coins who was known as "Le Diable d'Argent," the Money Devil.

In the United States, an anti-British campaign poster for James Monroe in 1812 depicted the Hartford Federalist

Convention candidate as the Imperial Devil.

The nineteenth-century representations of the Devil are more romanticized than the earlier illustrations. By that time, the fear of the Devil had greatly abated, and artists were no longer using diabolical drawings to promote morality.

La Magie Noire, a French manuscript, contains illustrations of the devil as a sleek, graceful he-goat and as Mephistopheles, the suave bearded prince of evil.

The demons were still represented with animal characteristics. H. von Gersdorf's *Feldtbuch der Wundarzney* typically illustrates some of the more notable demons. Baal is shown with three heads: one is a toad, one is a cat, and one is a king. His legs are those of a tarantula. Asmodeus is also depicted as three-headed. His heads are those of an ogre, a bull, and a ram. Amduscius is drawn with the head of a unicorn. Belphegor, who is usually shown sitting on a stool, has an ogre face, pointed ears, and a beard. He also has the horns of a bull or goat, the tail of a lion, and the clawed feet of a huge bird. Beelzebub, Lord of the Flies, is shown as a giant fly with fearsome eyes. And Behemoth, the demon of animal strength, is depicted as an upright elephant with a round stomach.

The Evocation of Demons

Although Satan was reputed to hold men in his power through the pact, there were sorcerers who claimed to be able to call up demons by means of a mystical ritual and to make these demons serve them. The rites were traditionally performed in an abandoned house or ruined monument, such as the eerie Tower of Witches at Lindheim.

A story is told of a very early sorcerer who evoked a demon and commanded him to remove his shoes. The shoes came off the sorcerer's feet so fast that he became terrified and ordered the demon back to the infernal regions.

In ancient Rome, specialists in magic evoked demons with incantatory poems. These magicians pledged their faith to the shades or to Pluto, the king of the underworld.

A thirteenth-century astrologer, Michael Scot, invited some friends to a feast. The guests reported that the food had been provided by demon spirits, supposedly from the kitchens of the kings of Europe.

The sixteenth-century sculptor Benvenuto Cellini, went to the Colosseum in Rome with a priest who specialized in calling up demons. The priest performed incantations and the whole Colosseum was soon filled with demons. They returned a second time, accompanied by a young apprentice. This time, so many demons appeared that even the priest was frightened. The others were utterly terrified, as the Colosseum appeared to be on fire from the brilliance of the demons. Before daylight, the entire crowd of demons disappeared, since demons are known to fear the light of the sun.

Many legends have been recounted about the power which King Solomon had over demons. The knowledge of the evocation of demons is said to have originated in the *Clavicule of Solomon*, a manuscript attributed to the biblical king. Scholars have had difficulty in tracing the *Clavicule* because it was never widely distributed. To make its powers effective, each sorcerer was required to copy the manuscript in his own hand.

King Solomon was said to have used a magic ceremony to assemble the demons and genii and to brand them as slaves with the seal of his ring. Legends tell of the demons burying books of magic under the king's magnificent gold and silver throne.

The death of King Solomon is only briefly mentioned in the Bible, in the phrase "he slept with his fathers." However, certain rabbinical writings state that he implored God to conceal his death until he could finish some work which he had undertaken with the help of demons. In order to appear to be still alive, he remained on his knees, leaning on his staff as if in prayer.

According to the Koran, the Moslem holy book, a crawling reptile was the first to discover King Solomon's death. The creature gnawed through the staff until it collapsed. Knowing that the king was dead, the demons ceased their work.

In the eleventh century, Leontius of Constantinople referred to these legends surrounding King Solomon when he said: "Had not Solomon dominion over demons?"

Gregentios, Archbishop of Taphar, told of Solomon shutting demons into urns, sealing the urns, and burying them.

Satanist Cults

Modern followers of the devil are known as Satanists. Their activities include Black Masses, orgies, the desecration of cemeteries, and murder for pleasure. The earlier Satanists consisted mainly of adult pleasure-seekers and neurotics, but recently many teenagers and young adults have found in these macabre groups an outlet for their desire for adventure and rebellion.

The theme of the Satanists is expressed in the "Hymn to Satan," composed by the Italian Republican Carducci, who attributed to Satan this motto: "With a goad of a restless aspiration, I urge men on until they outgrow faith and fear, until the slave stands erect before the tyrant and defies his curse."

The English aristocrats of the eighteenth century were morbidly fascinated with the idea of Devil worship and human sacrifice. In 1745, a nobleman, Sir Francis Dashwood, organized the Hell Fire Club, a Satanist group which was composed of upper class and titled men. At the meetings of the club, the men would engage in obscene ceremonies, naked orgies, and Devil worship.

As a prank, one member put horns and a black robe on an ape. He put the animal under the altar before the ceremony and stationed an accomplice to lift the lid at a crucial moment. The ape leaped into the air, landed on Lord Sandwich, and gave the entire congregation of Satanists a true fear of the Devil.

In 1945, in Warwickshire, England, a Satanist group cut the throat of a man named Charles Walton as a sacrifice to the earth spirits.

In Bedfordshire, England, the Clophill churchyard has been regularly vandalized by Satanists since 1963. Graves are broken into and skulls are impaled on a post within a circle of human bones. This suggests the Satanist ritual which uses the bones of the dead to harm an enemy. The bones are sprinkled with a magic powder called *mana* and pointed toward the victim or an effigy. The unfortunate persons begin to suffer a mysterious bruising known as "The Devil's Pinch."

On Halloween night in 1968, a North London cemetery was raided by Satanists. Coffins were opened and the body of a newly buried woman was impaled on a spear. One coffin was upturned and decorated with a black cross.

In 1969, a charred pig's head was found on the altar cross of the parish church at Stousted, Essex, England.

In 1970, the tombs in Highgate Cemetery were ripped open, and the corpses were removed to be used in black magic rites. Voodoo symbols were found scrawled on the walls of the larger tombs in the cemetery.

The town of Vineland, New Jersey, was surprised and shocked by a young Satanist's ritualistic suicide in 1971. A high school student, Patrick Newell, was known among his friends for his strange, intense interest in Satanic rites. He would hold secret ceremonies with other teenagers in which he would sacrifice hamsters by squashing them with his hands and rubbing the blood on himself.

One day, he explained to his friends that he wanted to die a violent death in order to become a captain of the devils in his next life. To accomplish this, he asked two friends to bind his hands and feet and push him into a local pond. The boys did so, explaining later that they never thought that he would really allow himself to drown.

After Patrick Newell's death, the residents of Vineland discovered that there were between fifty and one hundred Satanists living in their town, as well as several covens, or groups of witches, and several warlocks.

In the same year, a young woman named Kim Brown was convicted of stabbing an elderly man in Miami, Florida. She claimed to be a Satanist who had killed solely for enjoyment. She swore that she had seen the Devil himself during a ritual ceremony and was simply fulfilling his demands.

The Reverend Terry Taylor is a highly unusual priest. He is the high priest of The Satanic Church of the Nephilim Race. The Reverend Taylor and his congregation conjure demons to learn both good and evil aspects of life, for he believes that both kinds of demons exist. He defines a demon as "an energy force on the astral plane" and "matter in its purest form" which cannot be destroyed.

Taylor's church, located in Chicago, claims to be a center of "the oldest religion in the world" and traces its beginnings to the Stone Age. He believes in God as creator of the world and in two other, lesser divinities known as Lord and Satan. Satan is worshiped because "he was the only divine being who chose to help mankind, not suppress it."

A very different sort of Satanic cult is found at Anton LaVey's flashy Church of Satan in San Francisco. LaVey himself presents a demonic appearance with his piercing eyes, bald head, and goatee. Calling himself the Black Pope of the occult world, he dresses in the black robe and collar of a priest. Others refer to him as "that man."

Descended from Georgian, Roumanian, and Alsatian ancestors, he claims to have a gypsy grandmother who provided him with a natural introduction to the occult. As a child, his reading consisted of *Weird Tales* magazine, *Frankenstein*, and *Dracula*.

His work in the circus as an animal tamer and later as a magician's assistant gave him his keen powers of observation. He then learned hypnosis and began to study the occult.

Feeling more and more strongly that the Church was hypocritical, he decided that Satan was the real ruler of the world. He dabbled in ritual magic and held weekly meetings with his friends. When he discovered that his magic usually worked, he began studying the Black Mass and pagan ceremonies. He soon realized that his new powers enabled him to control people and things for his own ends.

In 1966, on Walpurgisnacht, the most important festival in witchcraft, LaVey shaved his head and formed the Church of Satan. He performed his first marriage before a "living altar" formed by a nude woman. The press was invited to the ceremony. In his first funeral service, he consigned the soul of a young sailor to the Devil.

The late actress Jayne Mansfield was reputed to have attended several sessions at LaVey's church and even to have been the living altar at a Black Mass. Shortly after, she was decapitated in an automobile accident.

A young man who was in the church with his parents at the time she was killed, claims that at that exact moment, the lights in the church suddenly dimmed. Later, at home, his father collapsed in a fit on the floor. When he tried to speak, Miss Mansfield's voice was heard, crying and saying that she did not want to die. She blamed the Black Mass for her death and called out to LaVey to help her.

Anton LaVey's Church of Satan has been characterized as a "horror show" or a put-on. Certainly it is the most theatrical of the Satanist congregations. LaVey's theme is the pursuit of pleasure, and he seems to enjoy his grisly life-style thoroughly.

Charles Manson's "family," which committed the brutal murders in California in the summer of 1970, had some of the characteristics of a Satanist cult. The cold-blooded enjoyment of killing and the slavish devotion to a leader suggest a group that was bound together by ritual and a mutual belief in evil.

The Devil's Creed

The Devil's Creed, which is the Lord's Prayer in Latin recited backward, probably originated in the eleventh or twelfth century. It was not necessarily used primarily as a corruption of the Christian prayer, but as a series of meaningless sounds which could be repeated in order to induce a trance state. The Devil's Creed would sound like this:

Nema. Olam a son arebil des
Menuitat net ni sacudni son en te.
Sirtson subirotbed
Atibed sebon ettimid te
Eidoh sibon ad
Munaiditoc murtson menap
Arret ni te oleac ni
Tucis aut satnulov taif
Murit munger tainevda
Murit nemon rutecifitonas
Sileac ni se iuq
Retson retap.

5. Possession and Exorcism

Characteristics of Possession

ONE OF THE MOST frightening powers attributed to the Devil and his legions of demons is the ability to enter and possess the body of a living person. Possessed persons have been known to writhe and foam at the mouth, unable to control the movements of their bodies. From their mouths, strange voices speak, often in unknown languages, sometimes uttering a stream of blasphemies and curses.

The demon inside the possessed person fears the power of God and the Church and causes the victim great anguish in the presence of prayer. A possessed person will be made to draw back when holy water is sprinkled, as the demon inside becomes frightened by its cleansing powers.

While the demon is usually invisible inside his victim, he manifests himself not only by his control over the victim, but by his ability to solidify into foul substances, which are passed through the victim's body as excrement, vomit, or even reptiles or lumps of coal.

Often markings or raised letters spelling out messages will appear on the victim's chest or stomach.

Causes of Possession

Different religious groups have different opinions on exactly why a demon chooses to inhabit the body of a particular individual. A widespread modern belief is that a person becomes vulnerable to possession when he becomes involved in the occult without proper training. Contacting spirits through an Ouija Board, automatic writing, or a séance opens that person to the possibility of an invading demon. Amateurish practicing of Black Magic is considered even more dangerous and more likely to lead to possession.

In earlier times, demons and spirits were believed to be present in common substances such as water, air, and plants. It was assumed that a demon could enter easily through the orifices of the body during such acts as eating, yawning, and sneezing. Daily exorcisms were enacted, such as covering the mouth when yawning, saying a blessing before eating, and reciting the familiar "God bless you" when someone sneezes.

During the years when witches were persecuted, witchcraft and the evil eye were blamed in cases of possession. Since witches were known to be agents of Satan, it seemed likely that they would be responsible for choosing his victims.

Exorcism

Exorcism is the term used for any ritual which is meant to drive away evil or undesirable spirits and to prevent any bad luck or harm which the spirit might cause. Exorcism of a demon is a complex and restricted ritual; there are however, many simple rites performed habitually by persons who are unaware that these habits are actually forms of exorcism. As mentioned previously, the practice of covering the mouth when yawning and saying "God Bless you" when someone sneezes are simple exorcisms derived from centuries ago.

The Catholic Church has many exorcising rituals and objects, including the sign of the cross, holy water, rosaries, scapulars, and the various saints' medals. The sacrament of baptism is actually an exorcism. The preliminary words which the priest utters in a baptism are: "I exorcise thee, thou unclean spirit! Go thou far from this servant of God! Come out of him! Hear thy doom, O Devil accursed, Satan accursed!"

The Authority of the Exorcist

In the early Church, the functions of the exorcist were separated from other priestly duties. Four minor orders of priests were specially trained to help possessed individuals. However, the cases of possession became too numerous for the limited number of priests to handle, and it became necessary for all priests and even women, such as St. Catherine of Siena, to conduct the ritual.

In modern times, in order to perform an exorcism, a priest must receive special permission from his bishop. Before requesting permission, the priest himself must insist that the possessed person undergo complete medical check-ups and treatment, as well as sufficient psychological examination to rule out the possibility of a mental disorder. If no physical or mental cause is found for the symptoms, the victim is investigated for possible parapsychological involvement.

At this point, the bishop's consent is sought, and he bases his judgment on the consideration of four types of symptoms. To be considered truly possessed, a victim must be heard speaking in a language which he has never known and has had no opportunity to learn. He must show signs of physical phenomena which are in advance of his chronological age. He must demonstrate a knowledge of past or future events of which he could not have known by ordinary means. In addition, he must display two or more minor symptoms, such as convulsive fits or the development of a multiple personality.

The priest himself must have witnessed these symptoms and, if possible, have substantiated the evidence with tape recordings and photographs. If the evidence is sufficient, the bishop grants permission for the exorcist to proceed.

Principles of Exorcism

Hans Holzer, the well-known psychic investigator and author, advises exorcists to follow ten rules when performing an exorcism:

1. The exorcism should not use force, either in the form of physical strength or of drastic psychiatric treatments.
2. The exorcist should be familiar with the history of the case, including the individual's personality before possession.
3. The exorcist, while remaining concerned and compassionate, should not become emotionally involved with the victim.

4. The exorcist must have a firm belief in his power to succeed and in the words which he speaks in the ritual.
5. The ritual itself is extremely important.
6. The exorcist should remember that the possessing demon is a complete entity, although a demented one.
7. The victim should not be made to feel guilty for the acts of the possessor. The two individuals should be kept distinct from one another.
8. Possession is not the same as communication with the dead, in which a spirit's voice speaks through a medium, but will not take over his body.
9. The exorcist must never hesitate or become afraid.
10. Energy and matter are interchangeable in the manifestation of the possessor. A possessing entity may materialize objects, then make them disappear.

Exorcism in the Bible

The earliest Christian exorcisms were those performed by Jesus as described in Matthew 4:24 in the New Testament: "And they brought unto Him all sick people that were taken with divers diseases and torments, and those which were possessed with devils . . . and He healed them."

Also in Matthew is a description of one of the well known biblical exorcisms. In this incident, Jesus met a group of demoniacs, who cried out to Him. "What have you to do with us, O Son of God? Have you come here to torment us before our time?"

A herd of swine was grazing in a nearby pasture. The demons begged Jesus, "If you cast us out, send us away into the herd of swine." He did so, and the demons entered the bodies of the swine. Immediately, the entire herd rushed into the sea and was drowned.

Early Exorcisms

Pope Gregory the Great told a story of how a nun became possessed. The nun, while walking through the monastery garden, had a sudden craving for a piece of lettuce. Plucking the lettuce from the garden, she bit into it without first asking a blessing. The demon, who claimed to have been sitting on the lettuce, entered the nun's body. A priest from the monastery was able to exorcise it.

In the Vysebrad Church at Prague, in what was then known as Bohemia, a priest named Wazlaga Kralizzea ordered a demon from the body of a possessed man. He offered him his own body in exchange if the demon was able to bring back a column from the Church of Santa Maria in Trastevere before the close of the Mass. The demon brought the column back just after the priest had finished the Mass and was reading the last Gospel. Angered, the demon dropped the column, which broke into three pieces, killing several people. The possessed man was freed, however, and the broken column can still be seen in the Vysebrad Church under a fresco which illustrates the incident in great detail.

A French Priest Battles with Demons

The Reverend Père Surin, a pious and simple Jesuit, was sent by Cardinal Richelieu to exorcise the demons which were tormenting the nuns of the Ursuline Convent at Loudon. He arrived at the convent in 1634 and spent the next three years in combat with the forces of Satan.

The most severely afflicted was the Mother Prioress, whose body was inhabited by the demons Leviathan, Balam, Isacaron, and Behemoth. Five years earlier, another priest Père Jean Baptiste Gault, had succeeded in driving out the demon Asmodeus. To ensure that this demon would not return, Père Gault made the demon write and sign a deed to this effect. This unearthly document is in the possession of the Bibliothèque Nationale in France.

Père Surin was eventually able to exorcise all the demons from the Mother Prioress in the presence of crowds which totalled thirty thousand. The two made a pilgrimage together to give thanks for her deliverance.

The Demon Which Could Not Be Exorcised

The seventeenth century is filled with cases of possession in England and America as well as in Europe. A story which did not have a happy ending was told by an anonymous author who claims to have been present during the attempted exorcism.

This case occured in 1677 at Great Gadsdon in Bucks County, England. The victim was a beautiful sixteen-year-old girl who was known to have an exceptionally pleasant disposition. Her father had become involved in a dispute with a woman of evil reputation. Shortly afterward, the girl began having strange fits. Her throat bulged mysteriously and a strange, rough voice within her issued blasphemies and obscenities. The demon inside her would converse with anyone and would answer questions.

This entity explained that he had been sent by two women to possess the girl's father, but was forced to return when he found the man in prayer. The two women then sent him to invade the body of the daughter.

The father gathered several ministers and friends together for fasting and prayer to evict the demons. While they prayed, two large bumps came in the girl's throat, signifying the presence of the demons.

One of the ministers called upon God to torment Satan for his blasphemies. The devil cried and said, "I will do so no more."

As the prayers continued, the devil cried and roared. Soon one lump disappeared from the girl's throat, and the minister felt that one of the demons had departed.

The other demon remained, however, and he continued to torment the girl. He would sometimes toss her around or make her unable to walk. At times, he would give her the physical prowess to resist the strength of men. When the minister attempted to have her read from the Bible, the spirit would become violent, tormenting her constantly.

The account of this incident was written twelve years after the alleged possession. At that time no exorcism had yet been successful in relieving the possessed girl.

Modern Exorcists

There are many priests who practice exorcism today. In Rome, exorcists are not unusual, and even in the United States there are a number of priests who are capable of freeing a soul from demonic possession.

Father John J. Nicola, an Italian-born Jesuit priest, is considered to be the greatest living Catholic expert on exorcism. Father Nicola served as the consultant for the film *The Exorcist*.

Monseigneur Luigi Novarese is the exorcist for the city of Rome. He and another Roman exorcist, Father Gabriel, are among the most authoritative modern exorcists.

Another exorcist of international reputation is the Reverend Christopher Neil-Smith, an Anglican faith healer. The Reverend Neil-Smith performs as many as five exorcisms a day and recently was successful in exorcising a member of the Hell's Angels motorcycle gang.

The Real "Exorcist"

The novel *The Exorcist* by William P. Blatty, was based on a true story which occurred in 1949. The victim was a fourteen-year-old boy named John and the setting was Mt. Rainier, Maryland, not far from Washington D.C., the scene of the fictional possession.

As in the novel, the first sign of the demon's presence was the sound of rat-like scratching in the attic. The scratching lasted for ten days; at the end of this time, the sound of squeaking shoes, marching feet, and a drum beat were heard under the boy's bed.

Later, when John was riding in the car with his parents and a paternal aunt, stranger things began happening. A lap robe in the back seat curled up spontaneously, and an invisible force pressed John and his mother together against the seat. When they reached the aunt's home, John's father found that the car key was not in the ignition switch, but lying under the front seat. One week later, the aunt died.

John's mother believed that there was a connection between her sister-in-law's death and the increasing noise in her son's room. One night, during this strange activity, the mother called out to the aunt's spirit by name, asking her to identify herself by three, then four, knocks if she were the invading spirit. The rapping indicated that the possessing entity had been identified.

On another occasion, the mother held a séance at a gathering of six relatives. Based on the movements of a table on which the letters of the alphabet were placed successively, the relatives confirmed their belief that the spirit of the aunt had invaded John's body.

During his possession, mysterious brandings appeared on John's skin. Objects flew around the room, including a bottle of holy water given to the family by a priest. Physicians and psychiatrists tested the boy, but could not find anything physically or mentally wrong.

A series of exorcisms, which lasted one week, were performed by the Reverend William Bowdern. On the last night, the boy fell into a fitful sleep and for the next five days appeared normal. The possession continued even more violently, however, and the boy was baptized in the Roman Catholic faith. The demon still refused to leave.

One night, Father Bowdern placed a chain of religious medals on John and forced him to hold a crucifix during the exorcising ritual. This produced the first signs of progress. Again Father Bowdern commanded the demon to declare his departure. As he spoke, the boy displayed unusual strength in a series of seizures.

Later that night, John calmly announced, "Satan! Satan! I am St. Michael. I command you, Satan, and the other spirits to leave his body in the name of Dominus immediately. Now! Now! Now!"

A spasm seized him more violently than any which he had previously experienced. The boy said, "He is gone" and returned to normal. Today he is leading a normal life and retains no memory of his three months of possession.

The Hebrew Dybbuk

The Jewish theory of possession is based on a belief in the transmigration of souls. According to this belief, the soul of a deceased person enters the soul of a living person. The transmigration is a cleansing process for the soul. When an unclean soul, known as a dybbuk, enters the body of a living person, possession occurs. The reason for the possession is to enable the dybbuk to accomplish something which was not completed in the previous transmigration.

Occasionally, a cleansed soul will enter into an evil person in order to redeem that person. In this case no exorcism would be performed.

Two rituals for exorcism exist in the Jewish religion. One is derived from the Lurianic school of mysticism, which was practiced in Palestine during the sixteenth century. The other ritual involves a rabbinical court of excommunication, in which the rabbi who heads the court threatens the demon with excommunication.

Present-day cases of possession are virtually unheard of in the Jewish religion. However, since the showing of the movie *The Exorcist*, at least one rabbi has been requested to perform an exorcism. The request was not granted.

Exorcism by a Tibetan Lama

Tibetan exorcists believe that in a true exorcism, it is not sufficient to cause the symptoms of the victim to subside; the possessing entity must be made to materialize. Norbu Chen, the only American ever to become a Tibetan lama, claims to have materialized a demon when he exorcized a poltergeist from a Hollywood, California, home.

According to his description, the demon had a large body with small arms and legs. It was substantial enough that those present in the room could see it, touch it, and smell it.

In the Tibetan belief, the possessing entity is known as a *ydag*. The ydag, a negative element, resides with a positive being known as *ydam* in another dimension of human existence. They are bound to this other dimension by their *karma*, or circumstances influenced by their actions in a previous life.

A person with a weak will can be invaded and taken over by a ydag. In the unfamiliar ordinary dimension, the ydag goes berserk, causing poltergeist phenomena or other symptoms of possession.

Ydag may be exorcised by a master known as a *gelong*, using one of the two rituals of exorcism, called *ankur* and *wong*. Before performing the exorcism, the gelong prepares himself with long hours of meditation and prayer. The rituals themselves involve further meditation, chants, gestures, and the use of sacred articles. The ydag is manifested, then bound in such a way that he cannot function in this dimension.

Norbu Chen is contemptuous of the Christian exorcists, whom he feels are more prone to failure.

An American Indian Exorcism

An exorcism was recently performed in San Francisco by a Cherokee Indian called Rolling Thunder. The Indian was contacted by the mother of a young man named Eric, who had been diagnosed as a hopeless schizophrenic. At the sight of a clergyman, the youth had gone completely berserk and had to be taken in a strait jacket to a psychiatric hospital.

Rolling Thunder agreed to help Eric's mother and asked her to bring him some object from the boy's hospital room. She brought him a handkerchief. Later, the Indian telephoned her to say that he felt that her son would soon be home and at that time he would come to help.

Within a few days, the psychiatrist at the hospital notified the family that Eric would be permitted to return home for a visit. At home, Eric received a call from Rolling Thunder, and he agreed to let the Indian try to help him.

Rolling Thunder was accompanied by publisher Robert Briggs and writer Douglas Boyd, who were interested in the case. Before reaching Eric's home, the Indian had the car stopped while he rubbed white herbs on the faces of the two other men to protect them.

When Eric greeted the Indian, he seemed to be two separate persons—one who feared Rolling Thunder and one who welcomed him. Rolling Thunder talked with the boy for half an hour, then asked the parents to bring some raw meat, a coffee can, and some water.

Taking some herbs from a bag which he always carried, he burned the leaves, which emitted a pleasant fragrance. Next, he carried the burning leaves to all the corners of the room so that their smoke might purify the room.

At this point, he asked the family to remove the pet dogs from the room. Eric's father brought the raw meat, which was placed on a piece of paper in front of Eric. Rolling Thunder asked Eric to remove his shoes and put his bare feet on the meat. Throughout the ceremony, the young man's feet never left the meat and his eyes remained fixed on the floor in front of him.

The Indian took an eagle's claw and feathers from his bag. Circling the room slowly, he began chanting in an Indian dialect, occasionally stopping to speak to Eric in

English. As he moved, he waved the feathers over the head of the boy, who cringed each time they approached him.

Finally, Rolling Thunder waved the feathers more boldly over the boy's head. Eric screamed and hurled himself to the floor, with his feet remaining on the meat. Rolling Thunder moved the feathers closer to Eric and began to sniff and make sounds like a dog. He appeared to go into a trance, which was interrupted by another scream from Eric. The Indian stiffened and spat a stream of black liquid into the coffee can from which he had been drinking. Eric shivered, then got to his feet and left the room. When he returned, he said that he felt "relieved." Since that day, he is reported to have behaved in a normal manner.

PART II

6. The Craft of Magic

WITCHES, WARLOCKS, and other occult adepts seek ways in which to reach the forces of magic for good or evil purposes. To aid them in this endeavor, they use special tools, herbs, incense, candles, incantations, and knowledge gleaned from the Cabbala, the Hebrew book of mystical teachings and comment on the Scriptures.

Cabbalistic Influences

Magic circles, pentacles, and the inscriptions on many talismans all have their origin in the Cabbala. The magic circles and pentacles derive from those said to have been used by King Solomon to evoke demons. The inscriptions in these circles, which are also used in talismans, are usually various Hebrew forms of the divine name.

Most often used is *Tetragrammaton*, which represents the four-letter Hebrew name for God: Yod, He, Vav, He. The importance of the divine name to the Hebrews is noted in their use of the same verb for both "to name" and "to give form."

Other divine names used as names of power in magic are: Elohim, El, Agla (Aieth Gadol Leolam Adonai), Shaddai, and Tzabaoth.

A serious magician or occult adept must become familiar with the cabbalistic Tree of Life. The tree is a chart of ten *sephiroth*, or emanations, which did the work of creation. The sephiroth are arranged into three triangles consisting of two opposing forces and a balancing force. The final sephira, Malkuth, represents the roots of the tree.

The ten sephiroth and the cosmic powers which they represent are:

1. Kether—Supreme Crown
2. Hokmah—Wisdom

3. Binah—Understanding
4. Hesed—Love
5. Geburah—Power
6. Tifareth—Beauty
7. Netsah—the triumph of Endurance
8. Hod—Majesty
9. Yesod—Foundation
10. Malkuth—Kingdom

One side of the tree is male and positive; the other side is female and negative. Each of the sephira is also related to a color and a planet. These relationships are important to the magician, who uses this information in conjunction with two other charts known as the Table of Intentions and Table of Correspondences. Relating the three charts enables him to determine exactly which materials he needs to work a particular spell.

Some talismans contain a number which is derived from the Hebrew numerological system. This number actually represents a word or name which has been reduced to its numerical root. According to this system, each letter of the alphabet is assigned a numerical value:

1	2	3	4	5	6	7	8
A	B	C	D	E	U	O	F
I	K	G	M	H	V	Z	P
Q	R	L	T	N	W		
J		S			X		
Y							

Magic Circles

Since ancient times, the circle, which has no beginning and no end, has been endowed with mystical properties.

King Arthur's Round Table was made in circular form so that no one would be at the head or at the foot.

Farmers of Europe would draw a circle in the earth around a flock of fowl to keep them from straying.

It is ancient belief that children can be protected through the night by tracing three circles around their bodies with the finger. The person who performs this charm should concentrate his power into his finger and imagine white light coming from it.

The wedding ring is a part of the marriage ceremony

because, as a circle, it has no end.

Witches and magicians perform their rituals and spells enclosed by a circle. The circle is a protection against the possibility of malevolent spirits.

The circle may be drawn with chalk or made of string or cotton placed in the shape of a circle. It may be cut from a piece of cloth on which the proper inscriptions have been made. If it is made outdoors, it can be traced in the earth with an athame, or consecrated knife.

Usually, the outer rim of the circle is approximately nine feet in diameter. About six inches from this, an inner circle is drawn. Between the two circles, the names of the power are inscribed; "Tetragrammaton," "Adonai," and "Agla" are the most usually found.

Four cardinal points are also marked on the strip between the inner and outer circle:

The East is ruled by the elemental king Gabriel. A glass of consecrated water (rainwater to which a pinch of salt has been added) is placed at the spot, which is known as the Station of Water. The sign of the pentacle, or five-pointed star, is made over it while saying aloud: "I exorcise thee, O creature of the water."

The Station of Fire is to the South. Michael is the elemental king of this point. A candle is placed on the southern side of the circle to represent fire.

The North is the Station of the Earth and is ruled by the elemental king Uriel. At this point, a rock or handful of sand is placed to symbolize the earth.

The West is the station of Air, ruled by the elemental king Raphael. A sprig of mistletoe may be placed here.

Inside the circle itself is the altar, which faces east for white magic and south for black magic.

In serious magic, the figure called the Triangle of Art is sometimes drawn to the east of the circle. This is a double triangle with the words of power written along the sides. The purpose of this triangle is to confine any evil being or spirit which may appear during the ritual.

Magic Numbers

Numbers as well as geometric shapes are thought to have magic properties. Three is a magic number in spells and rituals. Triangles are used in magic as a symbol of three. The Holy Trinity is a familiar grouping of three; the pagan religion also uses this concept. The Earth Goddess, worshiped by witches, has three aspects—Maiden, Mother, and Crone—and the Deity itself is composed of the Goddess, the Horned God, and the Maiden.

Three also represents the basic family unit of man, woman, and child.

It is possibly significant that most children's fairy tales portray groupings of three: The Three Bears, The Three Little Pigs, The Three Little Kittens, and The Three Blind Mice.

Many spells call for an action to be repeated three times, as in the gypsy love spell which calls for a candle to be pricked three times.

The number four represents the four seasons, the four elements, and the four tides. The witches' calendar shows four main festivals during the year. As there are four directions, there are four cardinal points on the circle. Although four-sided figures are not used in magic as often as triangles or circles, occasionally the square or the rectangle forms a part of a talisman.

The number seven is significant because there are seven days of the week, seven seas, and seven wonders of the natural world. A person who is extremely happy speaks of being "in seventh heaven."

The number ten represents the ten sephiroth in the Tree of Life and the Ten Commandments.

Twelve and thirteen are also significant numbers in magic. Twelve is considered the perfect cycle. There are twelve months in the year and twelve signs of the zodiac. Since thirteen follows twelve, it represents the end of the cycle and therefore signifies death.

Witches' covens usually have thirteen members. It has been suggested that this number was determined by early anti-Christian witches who meant to parody the Last Supper of Jesus and his twelve disciples. There is no evidence to support this idea, however, since the number thirteen has pre-Christian associations. It has also been suggested that thirteen may have been chosen as the ideal number for a coven because it represents the sun, moon, and eleven stars, or it may have been an emulation of King Arthur and his twelve knights.

Tools and Materials for Magic

The magic sword is used for drawing magic circles and pentacles. It should be made from planetary materials or tempered steel and should be engraved with the names of power. The sword, usually wielded by the High Priestess of a coven, can be used to consecrate a meal for the group. The point of the sword can be used to sever symbolically one coven from another. To cement the ties between covens, the hilt of the sword is used.

The wand, which conducts etheric vibrations, should be made from a hazel branch. It could also be made from ash, associated with Ygdrasil, the tree which binds heaven, earth, and hell. Oak, which has Druidic associations, could also be used.

The consecrated knife is known as the athame. It is sometimes used for marking the circle, for divining, and for consecrating.

The pentacle, a powerful magic symbol, is used within the circle during rituals. It can be made of metal or wood or drawn on a stiff white card.

The cord is sometimes used for forming a circle. It represents the umbilical cord which links the witch or magician to the Great Mother. The cord can also be knotted to use as a rosary for meditational purposes.

Incense is used in many rituals. The magician knows which incense should be used in working a particular spell. The incense has psychological value in magic; it is also supposed to aid the spirits in assuming a tangible form.

A gong or gavel is used by magicians. This tool helps to keep them from losing consciousness while in a deep state of meditation. The sound is also said to help in establishing contact with the astral forces.

Serious magicians always keep a drawing of the Tree of Life nearby while they are working. The Table of Intentions and the Table of Correspondences must also be referred to while they are working. The Table of Intentions lists various intentions in performing magic and the planet to which each intention corresponds. The magician can find the planet in the Correspondence Chart to determine the color, plant, metal, gem, and perfume which are associated with it.

A candle is used in magic rituals not only to provide illumination, but as a symbol of the flame of understanding and as an aid to heightened awareness.

A crystal ball is sometimes used to enable the magician to visualize any spirits which he has conjured.

Magic unguents may be rubbed on the body to produce sensations which aid the magician's powers.

Herb and Plant Lore

A knowledge of herbs and plants has always been important to the practice of magic. Each herb is used for a special magical purpose. A potion must contain a combination of three, seven, or nine different herbs. Some of these potions, first used by the early herbalists, were later found to have true medicinal value. Other herbs and plants were endowed with magical power through legends born in the imagination of early witches and magicians.

The traditional scene of a group of witches boiling herbs in a cauldron is filled with symbolism. The cauldron itself signifies the womb of nature, from which the herbs issue. The three legs of the cauldron represent the triple aspect of the Earth Goddess. The four elements are also symbolized: Fire is used to heat the cauldron; water is used to fill it; Earth yields fruits to prepare in it; and air receives the steam that rises from the brew. Clairvoyant witches used to read the future in the steam.

Witches and gypsies knew the medicinal or magical value of most plants of the forest and field.

As protection against sorcery, verbena, cyclamen, pimpernel, angelica, bracken, fern, broom, maidenhair, growndive, fennel, garlic, and agrimony were used.

Foxglove contains digitalis, which is a true medical cure for dropsy and heart disease. The plant was originally named Folk's glove, as it was thought to be the glove of the fairies.

Orris root is used for divination. A thread is tied around the root to form a pendulum. When the pendulum is questioned, it swings clockwise if the answer is affirmative, counter-clockwise if the answer is negative.

Henbane is a poison which pagans used to weave into head ornaments to protect the dead against evil spirits.

Willow bark is used to ease rheumatism. It is known as "witch's aspirin" because it contains acetylsalicylic acid, the main ingredient in aspirin.

The berries and fruit of hemlock are poisonous. This is the poison which was taken by Socrates.

Selago is made into a fine yellow powder that witches believe will help them to understand birds and animals.

Thorn-apple produces delirium and causes its victim to do a frenzied dance.

St. Ignatius' Bean contains strychnine, a poison and stimulant.

Cinquefoil is used to cure ague. It is also hung in doorways to keep bad luck and evil spirits away.

Haws are made into liquor.

Vervaine soothes rashes. This herb, which is sacred to Venus, may also be carried in the pocket or purse to attract a loved one.

Elder cures burns.

Orpine, or fernseed, gathered at midsummer, was believed to make a witch invisible.

Dandelion is used for heart pains.

Camomile and vervaine are used to protect against thunder, sorcerers, and thieves.

Periwinkle, known as sorcerer's violet, is tied around an arm or a leg to relieve a cramp.

Tea made from valerian can be drunk and sprinkled around the house to bring peace to the home.

St. John's Wort, which was originally called Fuga Daemonum, meaning flight of demons, was thought to influence anyone opposing the will of a witch. The Irish would carry this herb under the left armpit as an amulet of protection.

Traditionally, St. John's Wort was gathered before sunrise on the day of Midsummer Eve. The dew from the leaves was collected to use as an eye lotion. The leaves themselves were passed through the smoke of the festival fires and hung around a home to protect it against lightning and fire. Young girls would place a bit of St. John's Wort under their pillows to bring them dreams of a future sweetheart.

When dropped in oil, the bright golden petals of the flower turn red and turn the oil golden. This oil is used for soothing bruises.

St. John's Wort can also aid in winning court judgments and business competitions.

The herb received its present name because Midsummer Eve, when the herb is gathered, was changed by Christians to honor the birthday of St. John the Baptist.

Trees

The willow tree was sacred to Hecate, the witch-goddess. In the sixteenth century, the witches of Berwick confessed that they rode out to sea in willow baskets.

Rowan, the tree of life, guarded against witches and lightning.

The Druids worshiped the oak, which was sacred to Zeus, Thor, and Yahweh.

White Witchcraft

White witches of the eighteenth century practiced magic to counteract the evil spells of black witches. This type of witchcraft was also practiced by country people in Europe who wished to protect their family and livestock from the evil eye of a black witch.

One way to neutralize a spell was to burn a candle while reciting:

> Let this candle be her candle
> This burning, her burning
> This curse, her curse.

A well-known way to destroy a witch was to drive a nail into her footprint.

A witch's curse could be reversed by scratching her forehead with a nail to draw blood.

A hagstone, a stone with a perfectly round hole in it, is a protection against witches.

Many eighteenth-century homes contained a witch-ball, a glass sphere filled with colored stones to protect against witches.

In Cornwall, long glass tubes filled with colored pebbles were kept in the chimney at night to keep witches from entering the home.

The witch who could give people the evil eye was known as an "eye-biter." White witches devised protections against this.

Necklaces of coral protect against the evil eye. Red ribbons serve the same purpose for animals.

European fisherwomen hang tiny cowrie shells around a baby's cradle to protect it from the evil eye. In the Mediterranean, peasants use blue beads to protect children and livestock.

Peacock feathers are considered unlucky because of the eyes in the tail, which might give an evil eye.

To reverse a spell and burn the witch, hair, fingernail parings, blood, and urine from the witch are placed in a pot which is heated on the hearth fire at midnight.

In southern Europe, people spit three times or touch iron to neutralize a spell.

Mediterranean fishing boats are painted with eyes to counteract an evil spell.

A proverb says: "Eat then not the bread of him that hath an evil eye."

Witches' Curses

The easiest way to put a curse on someone is to make an effigy of wax or clay and stick pins in it.

Witches of earlier times were known to give their victims an apple or a piece of bread and butter which had been cursed by the witch.

Witches in Britain and Italy practiced the Curse of the Black Hen. A cake with black chicken feathers stuck in it was put under the victim's pillow.

Witches could sink a ship by immersing an eggshell in a cauldron.

"Anger powder," sold in witchcraft supply shops, can be sprinkled on an enemy's doorstep to curse him.

Love Charms

A love charm can be made with St. John's Wort by strewing the herb over the fire and reciting:

It's not the herb that I now burn

But ____________'s heart I mean to turn.
May he no peace or comfort find
Ere he bend to me in soul and mind.

A strange plant called a mandrake is used to work a Celtic love charm. The mandrake gets its name from the shape of its root, which resembles a human figure. In earlier times, it was believed that this root gave an unearthly scream when pulled from the earth. Therefore animals would be made to dig it up in order to spare human ears the sound.

To work this Celtic love charm, the mandrake root is dug up before dawn. The magician must be careful not to damage the root. He must also recite the incantation, "Blessed be this earth, this root, this night." The root is then taken home and carved slightly to make it resemble the person whose love is desired. The root is held in the left hand, while a pentacle is formed over it with the right hand. The magician then endows the root with the name of his loved one.

The mandrake root is then reburied, preferably in a churchyard or at a crossroad. A cross is formed over it with a silver object. One part of milk is mixed with three parts water and a few drops of the magician's blood. This mixture is poured on the soil with the words:

Blood and milk upon the grave
Will make ______ evermore my slave.

The mandrake root should be watered occasionally and visited every other day. At the beginning of the next lunar cycle it must be uprooted one hour before sunrise while reciting:

Moon above so palely shining
Bestow this night they sacred blessing
On my prayer and ritual plea
To fill ______'s heart with love for me.

The mandrake has acquired its magic power by now. After being dried out, it must be passed through Venusian incense and placed on a paper with a Venusian inscription, while the Magician chants:

This fruit is scorched by that same heat
Which warms my heart with every beat.

A silver needle or pin is then plunged into the heart of the mandrake. The magician projects his magical force through the pin. The root is then left on the windowsill in the moonlight until the spell works.

Amulets and Talismans

An amulet is a protection against evil forces, while a talisman is a positive force which brings luck.

Abracadabra is one of the most popular charms which can be used as an amulet or as a talisman. The letters of the word are arranged in a triangle:

A
B R
A C A
D A B R A

Hebrew origins have been attributed to this word, which may have derived from a combination of *Ab,* meaning father, *Ben* meaning son, and *Ruach Hakodesh,* meaning Holy Spirit. However, it may possibly be a derivation of "abreq ad habra" or a corruption of the Basilian word "abraxas."

A German amulet to drive away evil is written and kept in a private place:

SDPNQCN
DPNQCN
PNQCN
NQCN
QCN
CN
N

A talisman to secure a favorable court judgment is:

ALMANAH
L
MARE
AALBEHA
N
AREHAIL
H

A square containing magic words is used against conflagration:

SATOR
AREPO
TENET
OPERA
ROTAS

7. The Diviners

MAN HAS ALWAYS HAD an insatiable curiosity to uncover hidden knowledge. Those who are endowed with the gifts of prophecy and second sight are sought after by those who wish to know their destiny before they attain it. The popularity of divining is evident everywhere in our society. Gypsy tearooms flourish in every city. Card readers and advisers are listed in the classified advertisements. Even the small towns and rural areas have their "Wise Woman," such as the Egg Lady of Long Island, who reads the future in separated eggs.

It is interesting to look at some of the many methods which have been used for divining over the centuries. Some are still popular; others have faded into obscurity.

Numerology

Numerology is a surprisingly accurate method of divination. The numerologist makes use of the letters of the name and the date of birth to make his predictions. Each letter is related to a number which denotes its position in the alphabet, and these numbers are added together.

Serious numerologists have been know to change their names in order to find a name with better numerical vibrations. Since marriage gives a woman a new name, prospective marriage partners have been considered in the light of the new numbers which they will bring to the name.

Some numerologists believe that each individual's name was predestined because it is numerologically related to him.

Astrology

Astrology is an ancient divinatory art which continues to fascinate people of all countries today. It is one of the more complex and exacting of the occult sciences, as it requires some knowledge of astronomy and the movements of the celestial bodies.

Astrologers have attempted to discover a biblical basis for their science in the passage from Genesis which says: "Let there be lights in the firmament of heaven . . . and let them be for signs, and for seasons."

Catherine de Médecis was involved with the occult sciences and was particularly intrigued with astrology. Her court included several astrologers, such as Nostradamus, who predicted the death of Henri III, the necromantic sorcerer Ruggieri, and Regnier, for whom she built the famous astrological column in Paris.

Astrology is based on twelve formations of stars known as signs of the zodiac. These are: Aries, Taurus, Gemini, Cancer, Leo, Virgo, Libra, Scorpio, Sagittarius, Capricorn, Aquarius, and Pisces. The interaction of these signs with the sun, moon, and planets determines an individual *horoscope,* or chart. A person's sun sign is considered to be the sign through which the sun was passing at the time of his birth. These are the signs on which the general horoscopes found in magazines and newspapers are based.

In charting a personal horoscope, the astrologer also considers the signs through which the moon and each of the planets was passing at the exact hour of birth. Certain planetary combinations can signify favorable or unfavorable aspects in a chart. The sun, Jupiter, and Venus, are usually beneficent influences, while the moon, Mercury, Mars, and especially Saturn are undesirable.

In addition to the twelve signs of the zodiac, there are twelve *solar houses,* which govern various areas of life: The first house governs the self and individual action. The second house deals with money and power. The third house relates to intellectual and literary matters. The fourth house deals with parents, home, and property. The fifth house governs love interests, luck, and relationships with children. The sixth house relates to health and work matters. The seventh house deals with marriage, partnerships, and legal affairs. The eighth house governs sex, sorrow, and changes in life. The ninth house relates to religion study, and travel. The tenth house deals with job and civic matters. The eleventh house governs friendships, hopes, and scientific matters. The twelfth house relates to the hidden part of life—dreams, secrets, and enemies.

In a personal horoscope, the sun sign is always in the first house, and each successive sign corresponds to the successive houses. Thus, a person whose sun sign is Aquarius would have Aquarius in his first house, Pisces in the second, and so on. As the sun, moon, and planets move through the signs of the zodiac, the astrologer can determine which planet influences each of the houses. Thus, the Aquarian, who has Pisces in his second house, the house of finance, would be favored financially during the time that Jupiter is in Pisces.

To determine future events, the chart is *progressed,* or gradually adjusted to show the positions of the planets on the date desired.

Astrology has also been used in medicine, as each part of the body is related to a sign of the zodiac: Aries relates to the head. Taurus relates to the neck and shoulders. Leo relates to the heart. Cancer relates to the chest and orifice of the stomach. Virgo relates to the lower abodomen. Libra relates to the intestines. Scorpio relates to the genital organs. Sagittarius relates to the thighs. Capricorn relates to the knees. Aquarius relates to the lower legs. Pisces relates to the feet.

There are three main types of astrology: tropical, horary, and siderial. The most popular is tropical astrology, which produces the familiar horoscope chart based on zodiac signs. Horary astrology also uses the signs of the zodiac, but is a detailed study used to solve a specific problem. Siderial astrology uses the constellation as guidelines, measuring from a fixed point. While each person is assigned a sun sign, the sign is not necessarily the same as that assigned by tropical astrology.

Horoscopes can be charted not only for human beings, but for animals and even corporations or towns. In the latter case, the date of founding, or charter, would be used as the birth date.

Astrology was originally practiced by sorcerers. Today's astrologers include a wide range of individuals, from witches to businessmen.

Some astrologers believe that the stars predetermine the

course of a man's life; others feel that they merely indicate trends and possibilities. As in all of the divinatory arts, self-determination can play as large or as small a role as the individual wishes.

Chiromancy or Palmistry

The art of palm-reading is part of the lore of gypsies, witches, and Hindu wise men. Like many of the other divinatory arts, the origin of chiromancy may be prebiblical. A reference in Proverbs 3:16 may possibly refer to palmistry: "Long life is in her right hand; in her left hand are riches and honor." Job 37:7 has a similar reference: "God has placed signs in the hands of all the sons of men, that all the sons of men may know his work." Whatever the origin of chiromancy, the human hand, with its complex network of lines, seems a likely place to record man's past and future.

In the seventeenth century, palm-reading was a thriving business for gypsies. Life was uncertain and dangerous in those times, and any information was welcomed which might serve as a guide. The painter David Teniers was particularly interested in divination. Many of his paintings depict gypsies engaged in practicing their arts, including one painting of his wife having her palm read.

In the nineteenth century, Mlle. Lenormand, who had also earned a reputation as a Tarot card reader, brought chiromancy into the circles of nobility and royalty. As fortune-teller to Josephine de Beauharnais before that lady's marriage to Napoleon Bonaparte, she was able to secure a position for herself at court after her client became the Empress Josephine.

Mlle. Lenormand published a book under Josephine's name entitled *Memoires Historiques et Secrets de l'Impératrice Josephine* (1827). In this book she included detailed drawings which she claimed were the markings in the palms of both Napoleon and Josephine. Since she was known for her theatrical qualities, it is not certain whether or not the palms were embellished by Mlle. Lenormand's imagination to represent the facts after their occurrence.

Her most famous prediction was the one made to Josephine concerning her forthcoming divorce from

Napoleon. This prediction, which she made from both the cards and the palm, so amazed and upset Napoleon that he had the diviner detained by the police for twelve days, in which time he was able to conclude the divorce.

In her *Memoires,* Mlle. Lenormand characterized Napoleon's hand as "brutal and unattractive from a distance," but she claimed that upon further examination, "one felt oneself suddenly gripped by a keen emotion." She declared that "the hand of Napoleon is a universal book, that it will be centuries perhaps, before this book is reproduced."

Each line in a person's hand has a bearing on a particular aspect of life. The fortune line refers to destiny; the life or heart line indicates professional matters; and the line of the liver reveals the state of health. The palm clearly indicates the approximate date of death.

In addition to these main lines, there are lines at the wrists known as bracelets, and there are lines of percussion, which can be seen when the hand is clenched in a fist. These latter are the lines of imagination and generation; they also indicate the number of children that will be born to an individual.

The fleshy mound of each finger is called a *mount* and is named for the sun, moon, or one of the planets. Starting with the forefinger, these are the Mount of Jupiter, the Mount of Saturn, the Mount of the Sun, and the Mount of Mercury. The Mount of Venus is below the thumb. Mars rules the central palm, and the moon influences the side or percussion area.

Following the astrological relationships, each joint of each finger is related to a sign of the zodiac.

Additional marks are the ring of Venus, which runs from the Mount of Jupiter to the Mount of Mercury, and the Milky Way, which divides the Mount of the Moon.

Some palmists claim to see various figures traced in the palm, such as stars, crosses, and even letters of the Hebrew alphabet.

Rhabdomancy: The Art of the Divining Rod

The idea of mystical powers being contained in a rod is a very ancient one. The staff, the scepter, and the wand have been symbols of power in all societies since the earliest times.

The Old Testament makes several references to the use of the rod, which have been interpreted as forerunners of the art of the divining rod: Hosea 4:12 states, "My people ask counsel at their stocks and their staff declareth unto them." Psalm 125:3 says: "The Lord will not let the rod of the wicked rest upon the lot of the righteous." Numbers 17 describes the manner in which Moses laid twelve rods in the Tabernacle of Witnesses, each inscribed with the name of one of the tribes of Israel as a means of knowing which tribe should provide the head of the people.

The earliest use of the divining rod was to locate metals in sixteenth-century Germany. At that time, most of the mines in the mountain areas were located through the use of the divining rod.

The instrument used in rhabdomancy was a forked stick, preferably of hazel wood. The operator would hold it with the point downward. The rod would twist to indicate the presence of the metal which was sought.

This practice did not spread to the rest of Europe until 1692, when a French peasant named Jacques Aymar became famous for his skill with the divining rod. Not only was he successful in locating metals, but he earned a reputation for his ability to track robbers and murderers with this strange instrument. He was called by the police to Lyons to solve the more difficult cases.

This French peasant's notoriety made rhabdomancy the subject of discussion by philosophers and scholars. Two general theories were advanced to explain the divining rod's power. The more spiritualistic group believed that the power of the rod originated from demons. Since the rod would only turn over water if water was sought and metal if metal was sought, it seemed that a supernatural force must be controlling the rod. The more rational scholars, on the other hand, evolved a theory of "corpuscles," which were believed to radiate from the substance sought. The rod, through the sensitivity of its operator, would perceive the corpuscles of the desired substance.

In the eighteenth century, the divining rod began to be used more frequently for finding sources of water. In the twentieth century, rhabdomancy was used to find water in drought areas. A British officer, Major Pogson, was extremely talented in this divinatory art. From 1925 to 1928, he served as official water-diviner to the Government of Bombay. His function was to relieve the drought-stricken areas of the country by finding sites where wells could be dug. Of forty-nine sites which Major Pogson suggested, only two did not produce successfully functioning wells.

A modern theory has arisen to account for the success of rhabdomancy. This theory is based on the idea that a divining rod, like a pendulum or Ouija Board, must function as an *autoscope*, or device which records subconscious slight movements. Proponents of this theory believe that the operator of the divining rod subconsciously notes the factors, such as slight changes in the condition of vegetation, which would indicate the presence of water, and registers this through the divining rod.

The divining rod has also been used to answer questions, indicating a negative or affirmative answer by the direction in which it points.

Metoposcopy: Divination by the Frontal Lines

Metoposcopy is a method, based on astrology, of analyzing a person's character and future by reading the lines on his forehead. This method was first set forth in detail by the astrologer Jerome Cardan in his work *Metoposcopia* (1658).

In order to divine through metoposcopy, seven lines are imagined to be crossing the forehead. These lines correspond to the seven celestial bodies which were known as planets in Cardan's time: Moon, Mercury, Venus, Sun, Mars, Jupiter, and Saturn. The wrinkles which occur on the forehead are related to the particular planets whose lines they cross. Thus, a person whose wrinkles cross the line of Mars may expect a violent death. A person with a wavy line through Venus may travel by sea and meet his death upon it. Long, straight lines show a character of justice and simplicity; the more wavy or broken the lines, the more complicated the character of their possessor must be.

In addition to the horizontal lines which relate to the planets, some foreheads contain vertical wrinkles which may form right angles with the main wrinkles. These wrinkles can indicate that a person is a usurer, a courtesan, or a generally unprincipled person.

The face may also be marked with spots known as *naevi*, which are related to the signs of the zodiac. A naevi on the neck is related to Saturn and has different meanings depending on which side of the neck it occurs.

The science of metoposcopy is so complex that Cardan was able to include in his work at least eight hundred illustrations of the various possible combinations which can be read in the human face.

In spite of the diligence with which Cardan pursued this science, metoposcopy remained an obscure method of divination. Today it has been lost to the more popular methods such as card-reading and palmistry.

Divination for Treasure

Sorcerers known as "treasure-finders" made use of a gold ring which was suspended over the letters of the alphabet. The motions of the ring would spell out the name of the place in which to dig. When the site was reached, the magician would draw a magic circle and invoke the name of the demon who guarded the treasure. A black cockerel, a cat, or a dog would be sacrificed to appease the demon.

Physiognomy

Physiognomy was devised in the sixteenth century as a means of analyzing a person's character by studying his physical features. Various French writers contributed to the development of this pseudo-science which, like metoposcopy, was related to astrology.

In some of these works, types of countenances were made to correspond to each of the seven planets, including the sun and moon. Venus represented perfect features, a charming smile, and a fair complexion. A Martian face was rugged and square, with brutal features. A Mercurial face was beautiful and dark, with black hair. The moon was related to a pale, cold, and sad face. Jupiter marked a face which was noble and handsome, with strong features. The Saturnine face was yellow and gloomy, framed in black hair. Since few faces conformed exactly to any one of these types, each feature of the face was shown to play a part in illustrating a person's character.

Foreheads were also an important indication of character. A high forehead indicated sloth and ignorance. A fleshy, sleek forehead meant that its possessor was bustling and foolish. A long forehead belonged to someone of a gentle and quiet nature. A square forehead showed generosity and strength. A smooth, unwrinkled forehead indicated vanity and greed. A meager forehead belonged to a simple but cruel individual.

The mouth and teeth were also considered. A laughing mouth meant that its possessor was frank, but vain and fickle. An unlaughing mouth belonged to a steadfast, clever, discreet, loyal, and hardworking individual. Beautiful teeth meant that their possessor was upright and courteous. Protruding teeth were the mark of someone coarse and cruel.

Even the eyelashes had meaning. Long curly eyelashes signified pride and arrogance.

Noses were influenced by the moon. A long nose belonged to a person of upright character, wisdom, and honesty. The possessor of a snub nose was vain, untruthful, and unstable.

The hair, whether on the head or in a beard, was influenced by character. Short, coarse, bristly hair showed strength and self-confidence, as well as pride, arrogance, deceit and simplemindedness. A person with straight, soft, smooth hair was gentle, timid, and weak. If the hair grew to cover the temples and part of the forehead, its possessor was simple, gullible, provincial, and coarse. A square, curly beard signified brutality, vengefulness, and anger.

Although physiognomy as a science oversimplifies and overgeneralizes, diviners of all types use their intuition to gain some insight into a person's nature through a careful study of his face.

Phrenology

Phrenology, the science which relates the actions of the higher world to the human brain, was detailed by Robert Fludd in *Utriusque Cosme Historia* in the early seventeenth century. This became a popular method of divination during the nineteenth century, and even today, diviners can be found who will read the "bumps" in a person's head as a means of revealing his character and destiny.

Fludd divided the skull into several sections, each ruled by a sphere. The celestial sphere, composed of God and the angels, is believed to penetrate directly to the soul through the top of the skull. The sphere of perception, beneath the forehead, involves the four elements, which communicate with the five senses. The sphere of the imaginable world, which contains the sensations produced by the imagination, regulates dreams and hallucinations. Within this sphere are the "shadows" of the elements contained in the previous sphere. The imaginative sphere is linked to the intellectual sphere, which is placed at the center of the skull, by a curvy line, strangely known as a "worm." At the back of the skull is a sphere which pertains to memory and penetrates through the spinal marrow.

The phrenologist, by rubbing his hands over the head, notes the formation of the skull and relates it to the corresponding spheres.

Divination with Coffee Grinds

An ancient method of divination consists of interpreting the patterns made by coffee grinds which are soaked briefly in water. The diviner is required to say certain magic words during each step of this ritual.

When adding the water to the coffee in the pot, say, "Aqua horaxit venias carajôs." Stir the mixture with a spoon, saying, "Fixatur et patricam explinabit tornare." Then pour the coffee grinds on a white, unglazed plate, saying, "Hax verticaline, pax fantas marobom, max destinatus, veida porol." Allow the grinds to settle, and drain off the water. The future is read in the patterns formed by the grinds. Circles mean that money will come. Crowns represent political success. Diamonds signify good fortune in love. If a number is discerned, it should be played in the lottery.

The language used in this incantation was said by Swedenborg to be the language of demons.

Three Vases of Artephius

The Three Vases of Artephius was an ancient method of

divination in which the diviner "reads" the contents of the three vases entirely through his psychic ability. Precise preparations are needed to use this method. A table should be built on trestles in a lonely, high place. It should be enclosed on all sides with a wooden structure pierced with holes to receive the rays of the moon and the stars.

Three vases are placed on the table. One is of earthenware, containing oil and myrrh. In this vase, the past is seen. The second vase is of green earthenware or copper and contains wine. The present is seen in this vase. The third vase, containing water, is of white earthenware or glass. The future can be seen in the water.

Certain tools and the proper conditions are necessary for divining with the vases of Artephius. The diviner must have a wand of poplar wood, with half the bark removed, a brightly colored knife, and a pumpkin root. The tools and vases must be shielded from the sun. If the magic is performed in the daytime, the weather must be sunny. If it is performed at night, the sky must be clear, with the moon and stars visible. The weather should have been calm for three days.

Other Obscure Divinatory Arts

In earlier centuries, when divination was frequently used as a means of answering important questions, many minor divinatory arts were practiced which have since been entirely lost or greatly modified. Some of these methods were used to determine the guilt or innocence of those accused of a crime. Others were meant to procure the answer to a specific question. Still others depended largely upon the interpretation of the diviner and could be used to uncover a wide range of past and future events.

Aeromancy was divination by examination of the various and different phenomena of the air.

Alectoromancy, or *alectryomancy*, was divination with a cockerel. This is a very famous and ancient method of divination. On a very smooth spot, a circle was made which was divided according to the letters of the alphabet. A grain of wheat was place on each letter beginning with *A*, while a verse was recited which begins, "Behold the truth." A pure-white cockerel, with its claws cut, is placed in the circle. The order of the letters from which it would take the grain was believed to spell out the message.

The Emperor of Valens used this method to determine the name of his successor. The cock spelled out THEOD, which was interpreted as Theodorus, so the emperor had all men of that name killed. His successor was Theodosius.

Aleuromancy, or *alphitomancy*, was divination of guilt by the use of wheat or barley cakes which could not be swallowed by a guilty person.

Arithmancy was divination by numbers.

Astragalomancy, or *astragyromancy*, was a form of divination using knucklebones marked with the letters of the alphabet. These knucklebones were the forerunners of dice.

Ayinomancy was a divination determined by the movements of a hatchet which had been struck into a round stake.

Belomancy is divination by arrows.

Botonomancy was divination by herbs.

Carromancy was divination by melted wax.

Catoptromancy was divination by the reflection in a plate of burnished metal suspended over a sacred stream.

Catoxtromancy was divination by the reflection in a looking-glass.

Cattabomancy was divination by vessels of brass or other metals.

Cephalomancy was divination using a donkey's head.

Chartomancy was divination by writing on papers.

Cleidomancy was divination by the use of a key suspended by a thread from the nail of a young virgin. After the diviner recited, "Arise O Lord, help us and deliver us for Thy Holy Name's sake," the key would revolve if the answer to a request was affirmative.

Cleromancy was divination by drawing lots.

Coscinomancy was divination with the use of a balanced sieve. Objects in rotation were supposed to possess a diabolic quality. The Devil is called upon to turn the sieve by the incantation: "DIES, MIES, JESCHET, BENEDOEFET, DAWIMA, ENIJEMAUS."

Crithomancy was divination by corn or grain.

Cromniomancy was a method of divination by the sprouting of onions.

Dactylomancy was divination by the rings on fingernails.

Daphromancy was divination with a branch of laurel. If it crackled when burning, it presented a favorable omen.

Demonomancy referred to any form of divination which sought the suggestion of demons.

Gastromancy was divination by sounds from or signs on the abdomen.

Geomancy was practiced by throwing a handful of earth on the ground and divining from the pattern it made.

Gyromancy was divination by circles.

Hydromancy was divination by water. In one form of this art, the noise of a ring striking a pot of water was portentious. In another method, three small stones were thrown into the water and the ripples were studied.

Icthyomancy was divination using fishes.

Idolomancy was divination using dolls or images.

Lampadomancy was divination based on the movements of the flame of a lamp.

Libanomancy was divination with incense smoke.

Lithomancy was divination by precious stones.

Logarithmancy was divination with logarithms.

Macharomancy was divination by knives or swords.

Margaritomancy was divination using an enchanted pearl enclosed in a pot. To discover a thief, the pearl would leap against the pot when the thief's name was pronounced.

Molybdomancy was divination using melted lead.

Oinomancy was divination with wine.

Omphilomancy was divination by the navel.

Onomatomancy was divination using names.

Onychromancy was divination with nails reflecting the sun's rays.

Ovomancy was divination with the yolk of an egg.

Ornithomancy was divination by the flights of birds.

Podamancy was divination by the feet.

Pyromancy was divination by the manner in which objects burned.

Roadomancy was divination by the stars.

Scionomancy was divination by shadows.

Spatalomancy was divination by skin, bones, and excrement.

Stareomancy was divination by the elements.

8. Tarot: The Key to Life's Forces

TAROT CARDS, with their intriguing symbols, are an exciting way to enter the world of the occult. These cards are more than merely an instrument for divination; they represent an ancient tradition, a philosophy, and, to those serious students of Tarot, a way of life.

Tarot Cards and Those Who Read Them

The Tarot is a set of pictorial cards which can be arranged in a variety of ways to reveal certain aspects of the past, present, or future. While Tarot reading was once the domain of the gypsy or the village witch, these cards have passed into the hands of persons from every walk of life.

Today, students of the Tarot are everywhere. They learn their art from instruction books, from courses, and from more experienced readers. Some readers obtain their cards as gifts and begin reading them for amusement for friends and relatives. If their predictions are reasonably accurate, they often find that their list of "clients" grows steadily.

Some become professionals and begin charging money for their services; others become scholars who are involved with the philosophical aspect of the cards. These readers feel that the cards are truly magic, each waiting to reveal its bit of insight to guide themselves and others.

Wherever Tarot cards are being read, people will gather, fascinated by the idea of uncovering new possibilities in their lives.

The History of the Tarot Cards

Tarot cards similar to those known today were used as early as the fourteenth century, but the idea of pictures symbolically depicting life's forces dates back even further—to the early civilizations of Egypt, India, and China. Although these early cards were made from clay, the high spiritual level of these ancient societies was manifested in their mystical drawings.

Some occultists believe that the Tarot symbols were actually developed on the very ancient lost continent of Atlantis. Relics have been found on Easter Island in the Pacific Ocean which indicate that the Atlantean civilization was further developed in its knowledge of the occult than we are today. According to this theory, the Tarot, as well as other occult lore, was then passed on to India, China, and Egypt, which became the cradles of civilization.

In fourteenth-century Italy, Tarot cards were used for playing a game known as *tarocco*, which was similar to three-handed bridge. From this word comes the French word *tarot*, which is now widely used to describe these cards.

The gypsies spread the art of Tarot reading across Europe. Each gypsy tribe included a Wise Woman who passed on the knowledge of the Tarot to those whom she felt were worthy of preserving the tradition. Even today, gypsy tribes in many countries guard the Secret Doctrine, the essence of Tarot philosophy, only occasionally accepting someone from outside their tribe as an initiate, or student.

The Relationship of Regular Playing Cards and the Tarot Deck

From the ancient Tarot cards, the various modern decks evolved and, with a few changes and simplifications, the ordinary playing card deck came into existence. Like the standard playing deck, the Tarot has four comparable suits: Swords, or Épées, which correspond to Spades; Batons, Sceptres, or Wands, which correspond to Clubs; Cups, or Coupes, which correspond to Hearts; and Coins, Deniers, or Pentacles, which correspond to Diamonds. The Tarot deck, however, has fourteen cards in each suit because it contains two royal cards, the Chevalier, or Knight, and the Valet, or Page, which have been combined to form the Jack in the regular playing card deck.

The fifty-six suit cards of the Tarot deck are known as the

Lesser Arcana. In addition, the deck contains twenty-two cards known as Trump, Triumph, Atouts, Greater Arcana, or Major Arcana cards. These cards are numbered from one to twenty-one and each is a detailed picture with great symbolic meaning. The remaining card, which is unnumbered, is known as Le Mat, or the Fool, and corresponds to the Joker in the familiar playing cards.

Because of the similarity of the Tarot cards to regular playing cards, the regular cards can also be used for fortune-telling. Many readers prefer to use the Tarot deck because its symbols suggest an interpretation more readily, but an experienced and highly psychic reader can obtain much information from the ordinary deck. Unlike the ordinary cards, however, Tarot cards change meaning when reversed; therefore each card carries a range of positive and negative meanings.

As the Tarot deck spread across Europe, each country developed its own artistically unique Tarot deck depicting the styles of art and costumes characteristic of the country. Thus, the Tarot acquired value as art representative of its time and nationality.

One of the oldest decks still in existence is the Sforza deck, part of which is exhibited in the Pierpont Morgan Library in New York City. This deck closely resembles the modern Tarot deck. Other decks from earlier centuries can be found in the museums and libraries of Europe.

Today, two of the most popular decks in America are the Swiss Tarot 1JJ deck of Muller & Cie with French titles, and the English-titled deck designed by Arthur Edward Waite. In addition, many stores carry an Egyptian deck originated by French archeologist Court de Gebelin, and a very modern deck by John Cooke and Rosalind Sharpe, who claim to have received instructions for the design of the deck from Ouija Board messages.

Napoleon's Tarot Reader

With the introduction of the earliest cards into Europe, Tarot became a mystery into which scholars and kings of the Middle Ages delved with interest. Card readers were often lucky enough to gain favor at a royal court and were then in a position to guide some of the most powerful rulers on the continent. Napoleon, for example, placed great faith in the prophetic Mlle. Lenormand, who predicted many of the ups and downs in his dramatic career.

Mademoiselle Lenormand was easily the epitome of the exotic fortune teller, with her theatrical clothing and dramatic manner. Napoleon was known to have been concerned about the influence of this diviner upon his wife. On two occasions he had her imprisoned, yet he was persuaded to allow her to read for him.

Mlle. Lenormand belonged to the class of diviners who claimed to be truly visionary. For her, the cards were only a means by which she was led into a prophetic trance. This diviner was able to change the image of the Tarot reader from that of the gypsy or witch to the society fortune teller. Robespierre and Louis XVIII were among her clients, as well as other important personages of France.

After her came a succession of lesser known society Tarot readers who worked in luxurious rooms rather than in the dingy hovel of the witch or the Wise Woman.

Interpreting the Cards

Although the pictures and the titles of the cards differ slightly in the various decks, the basic meanings of the cards remain the same for most readers; they are the timeless themes which have been passed down from the early gypsies. Just as the notes of the piano can be combined in an infinite variety of melodies, the seventy-eight cards of the Tarot deck can be arranged to describe an endless variety of human experience and emotion.

The twenty-two Greater Arcana cards represent the broader spiritual and physical forces which affect a person's life. They are like the broad currents that run under the ocean's surface and are capable of affecting the course of a ship's journey, while the Lesser Arcana shows the small waves and ripples which have a less severe effect and can be more easily avoided or changed.

These Lesser Arcana cards represent the more worldly aspects of life-dealings in money, job situations, journeys, and quarrels. Each suit has its own set of characteristics which guide the reader in his interpretation.

Swords, or Epées, the suit in the popular Tarot decks

which corresponds to Spades, represents the upper class the aristocracy, and persons of dark complexion. The traditional division of the four elements associates the Swords with fire, the dynamic element which can create or destroy. These cards can mean strength, strife, or misfortune. They can show the courage, boldness, force, and strength of a person's nature or its authority, aggression, and ambition. The presence of these cards in a reading usually signifies activity, progress, and accomplishment. The Ace, the most powerful card of each suit, carries the extreme portent of the swords, hard-won triumphant success or humiliating failure.

The suit of Batons or Wands, which corresponds to Clubs, represents the lower class, the humble, the modest, and loyal persons. Wands are associated with the element of air and can signify growth and glorious enterprise. The Ace of this suit can represent fulfillment through creativity at its highest level or the frustration of one who has never been able to realize his goals.

Coupes, or Cups, which have become Hearts in the playing card deck, are associated with the element of water, for the cup holds water, which represents life. Like the familiar Heart, Cups are associated with love and with romantic or familial bliss. These are the cards which reveal emotional currents and can indicate romantic interest. Cups are associated with the clergy class; the cup pictured in most decks is the ornate sacramental goblet. The persons represented by this suit are kind-hearted and usually of a fair complexion. The meaning of the Ace of Cups can range from perfect, fulfilling love to love which is unrequited or has been rendered sterile and meaningless.

Deniers, or Coins, are, like their corresponding suit of Diamonds, associated with money and material possessions. Not surprisingly, this suit is associated with the merchant and business class, with persons of wealth or business acumen. Their element is the earth, in which the worldly treasures of gold and diamonds are found. In a reading, Coins usually express the ups and downs of material comfort and well-being. The Ace represents the extremes, from wealth which gives great satisfaction to its possesor to wealth which has corrupted its possessor and made him unable to enjoy its benefits.

Because of the large number of Major Arcana cards, it might become tedious for a reader who is not interested in becoming a Diviner to read the description and interpretation of each and every one of these cards. A short description of some of the most dramatic or interesting cards, should provide an introduction to this important section of the Tarot deck.

The unnumbered card—Le Mat, or the Fool—can be equated with the Joker of the playing card deck. Like the Joker, the Fool is a jester dressed in gay costume who represents the light-hearted, playful side of life. In its extreme, it can represent a foolhardy or irresponsible person, or even one who is so out of touch with reality as to be psychotic.

Card Number VI is L'Amoureux, the Lovers. While this card can be interpreted as the obvious, romantic type of love, it can also mean a testing of love or a reaching for spiritual love. The Lovers can also represent love of beauty in nature or in art. At its worst, this card can show problems in love or marriage, separation, or an unfortunate choice.

Number VII, Le Chariot, the Chariot, is just what it seems to be, a triumphal chariot bearing a victorious conqueror. This chariot can indicate the aggressive nature of an individual, a personal triumph over obstacles, or self-discipline which works to attain a goal. The negative aspects of this card are failure and defeat or a lack of responsibility, causing the loss of a goal.

The Hermit, L'Hermite, is card number VII. Following the nature of the hermit, this card can indicate drawing into oneself, seeking inner wisdom, or using careful discretion. In its negative position, the Hermit can show an excess of caution or the opposite, rashness and haste.

Card number X is La Roue de Fortune, the Wheel of Fortune. This card is important in a reading, for it shows a turning point in a person's life. As the wheel turns, it can bring good or bad fortune. The Wheel often appears in a reading to show a *karmic* influence, an inevitable occurrence arising from the pattern of a past life or lives.

Le Pendu, the Hanged Man, is card number XII. The suspension of the man from the rope represents life in suspension. This card shows an individual at a turning point which requires sacrifice and readjustment if it is to result in the accomplishment of an important goal. In reverse, the Hanged Man can indicate that not enough effort has been made because of laziness or preoccupation with ego.

Probably the most mysterious card in the deck is La Mort, the Death Card, which depicts a gruesome skeleton. Appropriately, the number of this card is XIII. The number thirteen actually signifies death in mystical terms because it follows twelve, which represents the perfect cycle. The Death Card does not necessarily predict the death of an individual in a reading. The death can be that of a relationship, a business, or a project. This morbid-looking card can even have abenevolent significance; it can mean the end of one era and the beginning of another, perhaps happier one. One very modern deck of cards gives the Death Card a new name, Rebirth, signifying the continuity of nature. In reverse, the Death Card stands for stagnation or immobility, which are the true opposites of death and rebirth.

Another fearsome-looking card is Le Diable, the Devil, number XV. Since the Devil is the symbol of black magic, this card in an upright position is almost always a bad omen in a reading. The Devil can indicate a condition of bondage, a weird psychic experience, or a shocking event. This card takes on a more hopeful meaning when reversed; it then becomes a release from fears and handicaps. The reading which includes this card in reverse can be showing an individual turning toward a more spiritual life.

La Maison de Dieu, the House of God, or the Lightning-Struck Tower is number XVI. This card indicates a dramatic change in an individual's life. Usually the change is the destruction or loss of something cherished, possibly an idea or relationship. However, the breakdown of one situation can open the way for a stimulating and rewarding change. In reverse the card shows the inability to change or to be rid of a burden. Like the Death Card, the Lightning-Struck Tower can be an indicator of extremely good or extremely bad fortune.

Number XXI, Le Monde, or the World, is one of the most promising cards to appear in a reading if it is in the upright position. As the world is round and therefore has no beginning or end, this card signifies the perfect completion of the circle, the attainment of the goal toward which the other cards have led. The World in reverse indicates the inability to complete a cycle which might have ended in success. Significantly, the World is the final of the Major Arcana cards.

Although the meanings which have been presented here are basic to most Tarot decks, each reader must interpret the degree of meaning which he feels will apply to each card in the reading. It is not enough to know the meaning of each card; it is necessary to consider the position of each card in a reading and to relate the cards to one another so that they form a logical sequence. The cards influence one another, enabling the reader to see patterns within the spread of the cards. The Death Card, for instance, is not likely to mean physical death unless the cards around it indicate illness or accident, separation and sorrow.

The Reading

As the reading begins, the reader is known as the Diviner; the person seeking knowledge becomes the Querent. The atmosphere should be tranquil. The cards are laid on the table or on the floor according to the circumstances and preference of the Querent and the Diviner. Before each reading, the Querent must shuffle the cards thoroughly in order to infuse them with his vibrations. The Diviner usually lays the cards in the direction in which he receives them from the Querent.

No one has yet been able to rediscover the precise method in which the cards were spread by the gypsies of earlier centuries. Each guide to the reading of the Tarot recommends several possible spreads which have been developed by experienced Diviners over the years. Some are basic spreads which give a general outlook on the Querent's past, present, and future. Others give specific information desired by the Querent. Readings can be given which cover a specific period in the Querent's life—anywhere from one day to one year. Sometimes a Querent is more interested in his relationship with others than in the details of his own life. In this case, the Diviner can give a reading which includes a character description of four persons of the

Querent's acquaintance and the relationships between the four persons and their relationship with the Querent. Some other readings include a short "yes or no" reading and a spiritual reading using only the Major Arcana cards.

Each reader usually finds that he feels most comfortable with one or more particular methods and may even modify these to the needs of the Querent. A Diviner who is truly relying on his psychic ability does not need to be given any details about the Querent; whatever is important will be revealed in the cards. In the reading involving relationships with four persons, the Diviner should not know the identity of any of the four persons involved. Usually, more accurate results can be obtained by reading for strangers than for friends and relatives because the Diviner is less likely to be influenced by information which he has previous to the reading. When reading for a person to whom the reader has a strong emotional tie, there is also a reluctance to disclose unpleasant news or unfavorable character traits which show up in the cards.

A very experienced Diviner can give the Querent surprisingly detailed information, often including names and places. Time is difficult to pinpoint in a Tarot reading; often a reader can only place an event within a six-week or even six-month period except in those readings which are specifically time-oriented. The experienced and highly psychic Diviner is relying strongly on the vibrations which he receives from the Querent to aid him in his interpretation of the cards.

Querents have often asked if their own thoughts might be influencing the Diviner through telepathy to see those events which the Querent hopes will appear in his cards. An influence of this sort would be difficult to detect, yet the Diviner who is thoroughly familiar with the cards would not read into them a message which was not indicated.

Experiences with the Tarot Cards

A young man is told by the Tarot reader that he will meet his future wife in November and that by June they will be engaged. At about that same time, a girl whom he has never met is having her future read by another method. She is told that she will meet her future husband in November and be engaged to him by June. The two meet in November as predicted; the engagement was inevitable, yet neither knew until afterward of the prediction made for the other.

A girl of sixteen is told by the Diviner that she will never marry her current boyfriend, but will be married before she is twenty-one. Two years later, the Diviner tells the girl that she will meet her future husband in the spring and be married before the end of the year. The girl meets the boy in April and is married during the summer.

As the reader develops his ability, he is more apt to see more than those common situations and can sense the character and emotions of the people who appear in the cards. Occasionally a physical description of a total stranger who is not present can be felt through the cards.

The Diviner is giving a four-person reading for a businesswoman who asks about four men who work with her. Without knowing their names or any other information about them, the Diviner lays the cards and the four personalities begin to emerge. Soon the Diviner can see one of the men as clearly as if he were standing in the room. She describes him to the Querent, who exclaims. "Why, that sounds exactly like Mr. ______!"

A beginning Diviner attempts to work a charm with the cards for three friends. She makes the charm by choosing the cards whose meanings suit the purpose and arranging them in an appropriate relationship to one another. Although her intentions are good, the cards were not meant to be used in this way, and all three charms produce the reverse effect.

Sometimes a person who is skeptical of the Tarot will ask to have a reading. Often the Diviner will be unable to receive any specific information from such a reading, for the Querent is blocking his vibrations. During one session, however, when a skeptic was having his cards read, the last card to be laid was the World in reverse. One meaning of this card is "Refusal to recognize the meanings revealed in the other cards."

When the cards have been read too often for a particular Querent, the later readings will become muddled and will make little sense. However, when the Querent truly needs help and the Diviner sincerely seeks to give this help, messages will come clearly and surely.

Some persons have had the experience of buying a set of Tarot cards with the intention of learning to read them, but lose the cards before they have a chance to begin. They buy a second deck and again lose it. At this point they conclude that it would not be lucky for them to begin Tarot reading at this time.

Others have lost friends by reading the cards for them. These readers find that their friends begin to fear their ability to uncover truths through the cards.

A Diviner who reads with ill will toward a Querent will find that his reading will not be successful or accurate. Tarot reading should be done out of a sincere desire to bring insight to the Querent. When a reading is going well, the Diviner will feel the glow of the communication which he has established with the Querent.

Events predicted in the Tarot are not predestined; free will is an important element. The reading is a guide, rarely an absolute prophecy. Being made aware of favorable or unfavorable periods ahead, of persons to trust and those to beware, helps the Querent to chart his own course.

Tarot Philosophy

The use of the Tarot to reveal knowledge through a reading is only one aspect of Tarot study. Tarot reading is not simply fortune-telling; it is Tarot philosophy applied to an individual in a particular situation. The Diviner who has studied Tarot philosophy and meditation can attain a greater depth of perception in his reading.

For meditation purposes, the Higher Arcana only is used. It is in these twenty-two cards that the essence of Tarot philosophy is concentrated.

Twenty-two is a spiritually significant number. There are twenty-two letters in the Hebrew alphabet and twenty-two works of creation in Genesis. The wisdom expressed in the Greater Arcana is also associated with the twenty-two paths in the Hebrew Cabala. As in all facets of mysticism, Tarot philosophy is religious in nature and the twenty-two cards of the Major Arcana are its highest expression.

In using the Tarot cards for meditation, the most positive meaning of each card is refined to represent a spiritual value; thus, the Devil becomes the forgiveness of one who has fallen, and the Wheel of Fortune becomes acceptance of what God has given. The emphasis is on a turning away from material yearnings in order to make full use of one's psychic energy.

Each card can be applied to counteract a specific problem within the individual. For example, meditation on the card of Strength can help to overcome temptation; meditation on the High Priestess can stimulate creativity; and meditation on the Lovers can bring insight into a relationship.

The meditation aspect of the Tarot comes from its Oriental roots. Meditation is an inherent part of Eastern religions, as it has been found to give the mind greater control. Transcendental meditation has been found by psychiatrists and psychologists to have a therapeutic effect on patients with a variety of emotional problems. Followers of the Tarot have found that Tarot meditation can give them greater assurance and tranquility.

Meditation, like prayer, is traditionally performed best in a peaceful setting. A yoga position is not necessary unless the individual finds it particularly conducive to relaxation. Some books recommend that certain meditations be performed indoors and others outdoors; the most important recommendation, however, is that the Initiate, or student of Tarot, must have a serious attitude and a sincere desire to explore the lessons of the Tarot.

When a person has meditated on, and understands the full meaning of all twenty-two Major Arcana cards, he becomes an Adept, or Master, and should at this point be an accomplished Diviner.

Very few who have ventured into the world of the Tarot have failed to be fascinated by it. The cards themselves appear to have been created in some dream world. The court cards and the personalities of the Higher Arcana have eyes that seem to be seeing into the past and the future. The figures have a solid quality, like statues, which makes them ageless.

Thus, the Tarot is not merely a deck of fortune-telling cards, but a whole range of truths, a philosophy, and a guide. Those who attempt to use their Tarot Knowledge to harm others will themselves be hurt; those who approach the Tarot with caution and a desire to learn will find that it can truly become the key to life's forces.

PART III

9. Necromancy: Raising the Dead

SINCE ANCIENT TIMES, man has been interested in trying to communicate with the dead. Speaking with the spirits would give a needed reassurance that death was not as final as had been feared. The spirits of learned and wise men were sought for the guidance which they had provided while alive.

Whether anyone has actually been successful in reaching the spirit world is a matter of controversy among scientists, spiritualists, and intellectuals. A growing number of scientists and other professionals have found themselves confronted by evidence which they are unable to refute. Whatever one's beliefs, the story of the exploration of the mysteries of death includes some fascinating episodes.

Necromancy was originally a practice of witches and sorcerers. The Bible says that the works of witches include "pretended converse with demons and the spirits of the departed." By this description, the necromancer who called the prophet Samuel from his tomb was known as the Witch of Endor. Samuel 28 describes how the woman was asked by King Saul to bring Samuel back so that he might consult him. Samuel appeared as an old man wrapped in a robe, and according to the Bible, "Saul knew that it was Samuel." Actually, by modern definition, the Witch of Endor was not a witch but a spiritualist medium, a person who could materialize spirits. Necromancers today are known as spiritualist mediums or clairvoyants.

Necromancy was practiced extensively during the Middle Ages, especially in Spain, where it was taught. In those days, sorcerers contacted the spirits by standing inside the magic circle bordered with cabbalistic symbols. The circle was a protection against the spirits, who were thought to have malicious and envious feelings toward the living. Pagans would attempt to placate the dead by burying valuable or favorite possessions with them.

The Necromantic Bell of Girardius

In 1730, a special bell known as the Bell of Girardius was used for raising the dead. Written on the bell are the magic words "Thetragrammaton," "Jesus," and "Adonai," a Hebrew name for God. Around the bell are the names of the seven planetary spirits: Aratron for Saturn, Bethen for Jupiter, Phulaeg for Mars, Och for the Sun, Ophiel for Mercury, and Phuel for the moon.

The bell was supposed to be composed of an alloy of lead, tin, iron, gold, copper, fixed mercury, and silver cast together at the day and hour of the birth of the person intending to use the bell. The bell was kept wrapped in a piece of green taffeta until it was ready to be used.

To use the bell, the person wishing to raise the dead would place the bell in a grave and leave it there for seven days. At that time, the necromancer would stand by the grave holding a piece of parchment containing the seven planetary symbols. This would cause the ghosts to appear.

Ghosts were known to rise from the grave spontaneously and walk abroad. A suicide would be buried at a crossroads, under a cross, with a stake through his heart to prevent his coming back to haunt his friends.

A wizard buried in Hereford, England, supposedly rose from his grave and spoke the names of several neighbors. All of these persons died within three days. The bishop ordered the body decapitated and saturated with holy water before reburial.

In Essex, a decapitated skeleton was found recently in a grave at the Cluniac Priory. The skull had been replaced on the neck, but the face was turned downward in the direction of Hell. The site of the grave is supposedly haunted by a phantom monk.

The Rise of Spiritualism in America

Spiritualism gained a new popularity in the United States

in the nineteenth century. The years between 1850 and 1900 showed the rise of some of the most colorful and skillful mediums ever known. Séances, sometimes known as "circles," provided an evening's entertainment for some. For others, séances were a lifeline to beloved dead friends and relatives.

Families amused themselves with Ouija Boards and table rapping. Many discovered that ghosts have a strong desire to communicate with the living world but have no means of doing so unless they find a person who is open to them.

The Medium and the Séance

People who wish to make a specific contact with the "other side" usually consult a medium, either privately or at a séance. A medium is someone who is able to receive messages, and sometimes physical impressions, from persons who are no longer living. Usually this is done in a trance state, but some mediums receive messages without losing their awareness.

The entranced medium usually works through a spirit guide or "control." This is a more advanced spirit who enables the other spirits to speak or appear through the medium. The spirit guide is often an American Indian, but can be of any nationality. Some mediums have more than one "control."

Certain mediums claim to be able to materialize physical objects from the spirits which have been contacted. These objects are known as *apports*, and the mediums who produce them are called *physical mediums*, as opposed to *mental mediums*, who only receive voices.

Another type of physical medium does not produce apports, but is able to levitate himself or other objects and to expand or contract his body.

In some séances, a filmy white substance known as *ectoplasm* issues from the physical medium, sometimes forming itself into the semblance of the communicating spirit. Attempts have been made to analyze ectoplasm in the laboratory, but the material always evaporates. Photographs of ectoplasm have been made, however, and some researchers have had the opportunity to touch it.

Sir Arthur Conan Doyle, the author of the Sherlock Holmes series, was permitted to feel a bit of ectoplasm materialized by the French medium Eva C. He squeezed it and was able to say that it appeared to be a living substance, but it shrank away from his touch before he could investigate further. Eva C. was extensively tested for fraud, as were all of the celebrated mediums, but no proof of trickery was ever found in her case.

Many mediums have been proven fraudulent, and even more were suspected of trickery which was never proven. Since it is easier to prove the existence of fraud than to prove its absence, it is extremely difficult to prove that anyone can truly bring the spirit world into the range of our hearing and vision. However, there have been a sufficient number of extremely convincing mediums to make most scientists say that, while they may not be certain that the spirit world exists, they cannot say with any certainty that it does not.

The Spiritualist Church

Since survival after death is one aspect of most religions, it is not surprising that during the nineteenth-century spiritualist revival, a church was organized which emphasized this aspect of the Christian religion. The Spiritualist Church combines a traditional Protestant service with a session of clairvoyance by the minister. Usually the church also offers individual spirit guidance sessions and faith-healing sessions.

The clairvoyance session of the service consists of "contacts" with deceased relatives and close friends of members of the congregation. These contacts are made with the clairvoyant fully conscious. Only the voice of the clairvoyant is heard; the spirits neither speak nor materialize. The whole session is conducted in a matter-of-fact manner pervaded by a quiet joy at the reunion with deceased loved ones.

The Fox Sisters

The Fox sisters were among the earliest mediums in the United States to gain widespread public acclaim. Their interest in the spirit world began when the two younger sisters, Kate and Margaret, were small children living with their parents in Hydesville, New York. The house in which they lived had a reputation for being haunted, and in 1848 the ghost began trying to contact the Fox family.

Furniture began moving in the night and mysterious rappings occurred. The family attempted to converse with the spirit by having it answer questions in a code of knocks. By this means, they established that the haunting entity was the ghost of a man who had been murdered in the house. He told them the location of the spot where he was buried, and later excavation uncovered a skeleton between two walls of the cellar.

After this discovery, the haunting became very dramatic. The death struggle was heard, then the gurgling of the victim's throat, and the sound of the body being dragged. Hundreds of people would come to hear the ghostly noises and to see the site where the skeleton had been found. Upset by these events, the Fox family left the house. The two sisters were separated, one living with a married brother and the other with a married sister, Leah. The spirit followed the two girls and changed its tactics to a form of attack in which objects were thrown around or displaced.

Finally, the sisters attempted to communicate with the spirit through rappings corresponding numerically to the letters of the alphabet. After this, the unpleasant occurrences ceased.

Kate and Leah, the oldest sister, became professional mediums and acquired a considerable following, accompanied by both attack and praise. Eventually, alcoholism and feuding divided the sisters and diminished their professional standing.

The Medium Who Aided Abraham Lincoln

Abraham Lincoln was very much interested in the occult, particularly in spiritualism. He was acquainted with a group of mediums in the Washington area and frequently visited their "circle." A physical medium, Belle Miller, is known to have levitated a piano on which Lincoln was sitting.

By chance, the President became acquainted with Nettie

Colburn, a young girl of twenty who impressed the Lincolns immediately with her psychic ability.

Nettie Colburn was capable of going into a trance instantly. She received guidance through three controls: Pinkie, a young girl, Old Dr. Bamford, who was Lincoln's favorite, and an American Indian girl, who referred to the President as "the long brave."

These spirit controls gave Lincoln advice which may have affected the course of the Union. On one occasion, Nettie, in her trance state, advised Lincoln to visit the front personally to give his soldiers a needed morale boost. She also advised him not to delay in publishing his Emancipation Proclamation.

On another occasion, Nettie awoke from a trance to find herself holding a pencil poised over a large map of the southern states. She could hear Lincoln saying softly, "It is astonishing how every line she has drawn conforms to the plan agreed upon."

At their last meeting, Nettie warned the President that his life was in danger. He admitted that he had received warnings from several mediums. Nettie left, knowing that she would never see Abraham Lincoln again.

Two Physical Mediums: Eusapia Palladino and D.D. Home

Two outstanding mediums of the nineteenth century were the Italian medium Eusapia Palladino and Daniel Douglas Home, who was always referred to as D.D. Home.

Eusapia Palladino was known for her theatrical manner, which often caused her to be suspected of fraud. She occasionally did resort to artificial effects in order to enhance her performance, which weakened her reputation, but she also produced some results which could never be proven fraudulent.

Through her control, John King, she was able not only to contact spirits, but to manifest a human hand or face. She was also able to make herself weightless and to levitate tables.

D.D. Home was an equally outstanding personality of another type. He was known for his sincere manner, which made others like and trust him. Among his friends and supporters were such well-known names as Thackeray, Tolstoi, Elizabeth Barrett Browning, Alexandre Dumas, Napoleon III, and Empress Eugénie. Home gave séances for Napoleon III as well as for Czar Alexander II.

Home also did not produce apports, but he was able to levitate and to elongate or contract his body at will. On one occasion, he was known to float out of a window seventy feet above the ground and in at another window. A large part of his credibility was due to his ability to perform all of his amazing feats in a strong light.

Leonore Piper

Leonore Piper was a fascinating and credible medium who lived from 1859 to 1950. Mrs. Piper, as she was always known to her public, received spirits both in a trance state and through automatic writing, sometimes both at once.

She first discovered her powers when she was eight years old. At that age, she received a message from her deceased Aunt Sara and she knew that the voice was from another world.

Her mediumship went through three successive stages; the third, and most important stage was under a control known as the Imperator Group. This was a particularly advanced and intellectual group of spirits who were attempting to uplift the human race by thoughts transmitted through automatic writing. Other mediums later received messages supposedly transmitted by these spirits.

Other deceased persons whom Mrs. Piper contacted included Bach, Longfellow, the actress Mrs. Siddons, and Commodore Vanderbilt.

Mrs. Piper was thoroughly investigated by distinguished scientists and researchers. To test her trance state, these men would plunge a needle into her hand, yet the medium would give no sign of having felt it.

When Professor William James became the president of the Society for Psychical Research in 1818, he made the statement, "If you wish to upset the law that all crows are black, you must not seek to show that no crows are; it is enough if you prove a single crow to be white. My own white crow is Mrs. Piper."

The Woman Who Spoke with the Composers

Rosemary Brown is a quiet woman who has been able to produce brilliant music in the style of some of the greatest composers of all times. She has had no more than a few years of frequently interrupted piano lessons and did not come from a home in which classical music was greatly appreciated.

The music does not come from her own creative mind, she explains, but is dictated to her by the spirits of the deceased composers. The first one to approach her was Franz Liszt, who appeared to her when she was a small girl and said that he would come back to give her music when she was older.

Liszt leads a group of twelve composers who continue to give Mrs. Brown new compositions to present to the public. The other composers who have appeared to her are Chopin, Schubert, Beethoven, Bach, Brahms, Schumann, Debussy, Grieg, Berlioz, Rachmaninoff, and Monteverdi. Recordings have already been made of some of the music they have given her.

The composers appear as living persons, and Mrs. Brown, who has seen ghosts since early childhood, converses with them as easily as with the living. Liszt sometimes acts as an interpreter, as some of the composers do not speak English well, although they have improved their use of the language after death. Mrs. Brown says that the spirits have explained to her that they are able to continue learning even in their disembodied state.

The composers do not transmit music in this way merely to give more of their talent to the listening public. The music is a message, explained the spirit of the English musician and composer Sir Donald Tovey. It is a sign that life exists after death. In making public the new music of the composers, Rosemary Brown attempts to convey her belief in the existence of these spirits.

Liszt explained to her at one time that she had promised in a previous life to involve herself in this mission. Her situation in the present life was planned to make her as receptive as possible. She was not born into a musical family or given more opportunity for musical education because the composers felt that a musician with a career of her own would have been less willing to spend so much time passively transmitting someone else's work.

It was also planned that Mrs. Brown would have a difficult life in order to enable her to develop the sensitivity necessary for mediumship. On two occasions, however, when she was in a desperate financial situation, Liszt was able to ease her problem by appearing to her and suggesting that she enter the football pool. She won both times.

Rosemary Brown has been investigated by Leonard Bernstein as wellaas by psychic researchers, by *Life* magazine, and by the British Broadcasting Company. The details of her life were checked out to verify that she could not have had an extensive musical background.

No explanation, other than the one which she herself provides, has yet been found to explain the unexplainable Rosemary Brown.

Mae West Summons the Spirits

David St. Clair describes in *The Psychic World of California* how the famous movie queen Mae West became interested in spiritualism after meeting the Reverend Kelly, who amazed her with his accurate statements about her. Deciding to develop her own psychic abilities, she obtained from the Reverend Kelly the name of a medium who could teach her to meditate.

Miss West was pleased with the progress that she made, and she gradually learned to meditate for up to fifteen minutes daily. One morning, she awoke to hear a voice coming from her solar plexus. The medium told her that this spirit, named Juliet, appeared when people were making progress.

Later, the actress heard a man's voice coming from inside her. He was speaking in an old-fashioned manner, using the forms "thee" and "thou." Another morning, she was awakened by a group of men standing around her bed attempting to communicate with her. They were dressed in old-fashioned costumes and she was unable to understand their speech.

They reappeared several times, until the actress, tired of losing sleep, told them politely but firmly to leave so that she could get her rest.

Mae West's sister, Beverly, is a psychic who reads auras.

The Ouija Board

The Ouija Board is usually made from a flat rectangle of heavy cardboard with the letters of the alphabet, the numbers zero through nine and the words "yes," "no," "maybe," and "good-bye." The name "ouija" comes from the French *oui* and the German *ja*, both meaning "yes." A curved piece of plastic is used as an indicator. Usually two persons work together to attempt to receive a message from the spirits. One person could do this alone; however, with two participants there is less chance of having a single influence subconsciously manipulating the indicator.

The ouija board is one of the devices which has been called an *autoscope*, or recorder of minute unconscious movements. Psychiatrists sometimes believe that the messages received through the Ouija Board are no more than an expression of subconscious thoughts.

To operate the Ouija Board, each participant places his fingertips on the indicator and waits for it to move. It can move from letter to letter, spelling out words, give numerical information, or answer "yes" or "no" to a question. When the indicator tip rests on the word "good-bye," the participants know that the message is finished and the spirits have departed.

Spirits of the Ouija Board

The Ouija Board provides a fertile field for those who wish to contact the spirits. Many persons who have sought an occult experience by this means have found themselves drawn into a fascinating, but ultimately terrifying, experience. A few individuals claim to have been successful in contacting well-known or highly interesting spirit personalities. These persons have publicized their experiences in order to substantiate the existence of the spirit world.

One victim of a terrifying Ouija Board experience is Alan Vaughan, author of *Patterns of Prophecy*. Playing with the board to amuse a sick friend, the first message he received was a warning of a flood in New York in 1973. Immediately after this, the radio announced that Dorothy Kilgallen, the columnist, had died of a heart attack. Mr. Vaughan and his friend asked the Ouija Board if this was true. The answer came that her death was actually from poisoning. Later, the papers announced that the columnist had died from a combination of alcohol and barbiturates.

Two spirits appeared to Vaughan through the Ouija Board as distinct personalities. The spirit called "Z" had an old-fashioned vocabulary. When Vaughan experimented alone with the Ouija Board, a spirit named "Nada" (which incidentally is the Spanish word for "nothing") came through. She gave details of her life and began to haunt the author until he felt her presence inside his head. He felt that she was jealous that he was alive while she must remain disembodied.

In an effort to free himself from this spirit, Vaughan attempted to receive a message from "Z" with the help of a friend. The message came: "Awful consequences—possession."

Still using the board, Vaughan tried to discover how to avoid the consequences. The board spelled only nonsense, while the spirits of "Nada" and "Z" seemed to be pressing on his brain. Finally, the spirits asked him to write with a pencil. The message which appeared was, "Each of us has a spirit while living. Do not meddle with the spirits of the dead."

Mr. Vaughan reports that he felt energy rising through his body and pushing out the spirits, while his mind expanded to infinity. After recovering from this experience, he threw away the Ouija Board.

An interesting Ouija Board "professional" is Hester Travers-Smith, who always operates the board alone and receives messages with lightening speed. Her board has spirit "controls" that operate as at a séance to introduce the other spirits. She received many interesting communications from Oscar Wilde, which she recorded in a book, *Psychic Messages of Oscar Wilde*. She also received a description of the sinking of the *Lusitania* from Sir Hugh Lane, shortly after his death in the disaster.

The most lengthy Ouija Board phenomenon began with the emergence of Patience Worth in 1912 through a Ouija Board operated by a St. Louis housewife, Mrs. Pearl Curran.

Patience Worth is a spirit who claims to have lived in seventeenth-century England and migrated to America as an adult. Several statements which she made concerning her home and environment were later verified.

Her speech showed her to be a very literate and witty personality. Through Mrs. Curran's Ouija Board, she dictated six novels, which are considered excellent by many literary critics. One, *The Sorry Tale*, is an account of the life and times of Jesus Christ. The spirit wrote so prolifically that a publication called *Patience Worth's Magazine* was started to handle her work.

Mrs. Curran, through whom these literary works were created, had only an eighth-grade education and was known to have traveled very little.

Automatic Writing

To contact the spirits through automatic writing, the psychic holds a pencil over the paper and waits for his hand to begin moving. Persons who have witnessed automatic writing have been amazed at the distinct impression that the pencil is manipulated by an unseen force.

Many persons who practice automatic writing receive the signatures of famous people. Baron Guldenstubbe, who originated the idea of automatic writing in the nineteenth century, claims to have produced the signatures of Pierre Abelard, Heloise, and Julius and Augustus Caesar.

The wife of poet W.B. Yeats was able to produce automatic writing.

The French author Victor Hugo, who became intensely interested in communicating with the spirits through table-rapping, also produced automatic writing. He received a spirit which signed itself as the "Ass of Balaam."

The Ghost inside the Living

The newest frontier in necromancy is the evocation of the ghost inside the living, more properly known as the *etheric body* or *shadow being*. Experiments in releasing the transparent body from the physical body, in a feat known as *astral projection*, are enabling researchers to increase their knowledge of the fascinating world of the hereafter.

Persons who have highly developed their mental control can enter and leave their bodies at will and can choose the destination of their out-of-body walk. Many of these persons have said that they can go at will to a paradise—a place of unusual beauty unlike anything which they have experienced on earth.

The American Society for Psychical Research uses these people to test the validity of astral projection. The subject is placed in a well-lighted room with several observers. He is then asked to project himself to a specific place and to observe his surroundings carefully. The persons in the room with him are not given any information about the place to be observed in order to prevent their communicating with the subject through telepathy.

The results of these tests have surprised scientists and given them reason to believe that there is a "ghost" inside the living.

If the existence of the spirit can be proven scientifically, this knowledge will strengthen the religious views of life after death and the immortal soul. And if there are ghosts inside the living, we can envision an invisible population of spirits who have left the boundaries of their lifeless physical bodies and are making themselves known to those who wish to see and hear them.

10. Poltergeists: Devils or Innocents?

POLTERGEISTS are often confused with ghosts. Like a ghost, a poltergeist can haunt a house and affect its surroundings in a strange manner. There are certain characteristics, however, which are peculiar to poltergeist activity.

The word "poltergeist" itself means "noisy spirit." The name is apt, since the presence of a poltergeist is accompanied by loud, persistent noise. This noise can be rapping, thumping, scratching, or the pealing of bells.

Flying objects are the trademark of the poltergeist. Objects rise up and float around the room or hurl themselves into the room as if thrown by an unseen hand. Observers have noted that these objects often fly on a curve. They rarely strike anyone and never cause an injury. The objects never roll after landing on the ground. Glass objects often fly around violently without breaking.

Sometimes a poltergeist incident involves stones that are thrown at a house or other building. In these cases, the stones are always found to be unlike any which are commonly known to the area.

Poltergeists have also been known to start fires. Usually these fires are small and scattered throughout the building or area.

An important factor in poltergeist activity, and one which was completely ignored in the earlier cases, is the presence of a child or youth in the vicinity of the disturbance. The presence of this young person has been the most important aspect of the more recent cases. Psychic researchers believe that poltergeist activity is produced by a force known as psychokinetic energy, which is possessed by certain young persons between the ages of about ten and nineteen. Persons having psychokinetic ability have the power to control the movement of physical objects, with or without conscious knowledge. Proponents of this theory believe that when a young person with this ability is unhappy or emotionally confused, his psychokinetic ability begins to work, causing the poltergeist activity. The psychoanalyst Nandor Fodor describes this type of person as one who "may have suffered early in life a devastating shock that caused a kind of psychic lobotomy."

Those who believe that spirits play a role in the poltergeist phenomenon claim that a person with psychokinetic ability may unconsciously join forces with a ghost, thus causing some of the more outrageous poltergeist activities.

In the early cases described below, the poltergeist disturbances are attributed to the forces of the Devil; the child or young adult who may have been the agent is mentioned only briefly.

The Poltergeist of Epworth Rectory

Epworth Rectory was the home of the parents of John Wesley, the famous founder of the Methodist Church. Although he was not living at home at the time of the poltergeist activity, he discussed the phenomenon frequently in his correspondence with his family.

The poltergeist made its appearance in 1719, a year in which the Wesley family was involved in a controversy over the new prayers for the king which had recently become part of the family ritual. Mr. Wesley firmly insisted upon including these prayers, which Mrs. Wesley found offensive to her more conservative religious ideas.

The poltergeist apparently agreed with her, for the strange rappings and knockings always grew loudest during these controversial prayers. The noises would occur at all hours of the day and night, frightening all the Wesley children except teen-age Hetty, who always slept through the poltergeist activity. Her face would flush and her breathing would grow heavy at times, but she would not awaken.

Members of the family would attempt to converse with the poltergeist by asking it to reply in a code of knocks. It would always reply, usually agreeing to whatever was suggested. It could also repeat any pattern of raps and knocks that it was asked to copy.

An unusual feature of the Epworth poltergeist was the mysterious appearance of a small fuzzy animal. On its first appearance, the servants reported seeing an animal "like a hare" race out of the kitchen and disappear. Later, the children claimed to have seen a small badger-like animal run out from under one of the beds. The children enjoyed the animal, which appeared a few times, and gave it the name "Jeff."

The choice of this name is interesting, as there were two previous cases of spirits known by that name: one was a talking mongoose who called himself "Jeff"; the other was a ghost known as "Old Jeffrey."

Each appearance of the poltergeist was accompanied by strange, animal-like noises. This type of noise was typical of the early poltergeist cases. It is interesting to note that in certain cases of alleged demonic possession, animal-like noises occurred in the victim's home shortly before the onset of the other symptoms.

The Woodstock Poltergeist

The account of the Woodstock poltergeist incident was published in 1660 in a British magazine under the title "The Just Devil of Woodstock." It was written by the Woodstock minister and schoolmaster, who had heard of the events directly from the men who had been present.

The incident involved a group of commissioners who had been sent to survey the manors and houses belonging to the king. The survey included a certain house in the town of Woodstock, England.

About midnight of their first night at Woodstock, the commissioners were awakened by a knocking at the door of the presence chamber, which they were using as an office. The door opened by itself and an invisible presence was heard to enter with heavy footsteps. The footsteps entered the bedroom, walked around the room, and went under the bed in which two of the commissioners were lying. The men heard and felt the mattress being torn apart and the entire bed pushed up from beneath. Presently, the room became quiet as "it" moved on to the servants' room, where it repeated the disturbance to the beds.

For the next two nights, the poltergeist activity followed the same pattern. On the fourth night, it grew more violent. Pots and plans flew around the bedroom and sounds were heard as though someone were beating on all the doors and walls. On the seventh night, in addition to the flying objects, the commissioners heard the sound of a fire crackling and men groaning. An investigation of the house showed that there was no fire and that all the men were quiet.

On the ninth night, a lawyer who was the brother of one of the commissioners, Captain Crook, came to stay with the men. The presence entered the room in which the brothers were sleeping, put out the fire, and threw objects around. Another commissioner, Captain Cockaine, left his bed to see to the safety of the brothers. When he returned to his own bed, he found it filled with the three dozen trenchers from which the men had been eating their meals.

The next night, the heavy footsteps were heard again, causing the beds to shake. The officers covered themselves with their blankets to keep from being injured by the flying objects which had begun sailing around the room. Around them, they heard sounds which appeared to be pebbles raining down from the ceiling. When the noise ceased, Captain Cockaine lit a candle, which was instantly blown out. In the brief instant of light, he was able to see that the room was strewn with tiny pieces of broken glass. After that night, Captain Crook's lawyer brother left the house, declaring that no amount of money would induce him to stay.

The next night, stones were heard flying around the room. When the officers examined these stones, they saw that they were not typical of those usually found in the area. The following night, the stones mysteriously disappeared.

Several nights later, the Captains asked the keeper of the ordinary, the abbot's residence, to stay with them, accompanied by another man as well as a huge mastiff. The disturbance grew so great that night that the dog became afraid and crawled into one of the beds. Stones and horses' bones were flying in through all the windows, occasionally striking, but not injuring, some of the officers.

Captain Cockaine and another officer, Captain Hart, called out: "In the Name of the Father, Son, and Holy Ghost, What are you? What would you have? What have we done that you disturb us?" There was silence, and the officers returned to bed.

Soon the noises began again, the candles and fire were put out, and foul-smelling water was thrown upon the beds. The "thing" crept under the beds and threw them to the ceiling with the officers still lying in them. The men were so greatly upset that they gathered together in the presence chamber to pray and sing hymns all night. During that time, there was no disturbance in the room itself, but noises could be heard at a distance, as of wolves kept at bay.

Shortly after, the evaluations were completed and the commissioners were able to depart from Woodstock. Later, many people spent the night in the same house, but the poltergeist activity never recurred.

In the first account of the events at Woodstock, no mention is made of any child or youth whose psychokinetic ability may have been responsible for the poltergeist. However, an account written in 1747 by an anonymous author reveals that a young man named Joseph Collins, known as "Funny Joe," had been a servant to the commissioners at Woodstock. This Joseph Collins had claimed to have created the disturbances to the officers as a huge practical joke. If the events truly occurred as stated in the original account, it seems unlikely that one young man could consciously sustain such a varied and persistent assault. According to the psychokinetic theory, it is possible that Joe Collins had played a few minor pranks, which activated his psychokinetic ability to cause the true poltergeist activity. Since the later account was never verified, however, any theories concerning the "Just Devil of Woodstock" can only be speculation.

The seventeenth and eighteenth centuries produced many accounts of poltergeist activity similar to the events at Woodstock and at Epworth Rectory. As far away as Iceland, a phenomenon known as the Devil of Hjalta-Stad terrified the natives of that country. Most of the cases involved bed-shaking, loud noises, and, most strikingly, a strong reaction to prayer. In all of these cases, the entity responsible was referred to as a demon or devil. It is possibly significant that this type of poltergeist case was seen in England at about the same time that the Salem witch persecution was taking place in America.

Bell Ringing

In the nineteenth century, a different type of poltergeist activity was observed. This was known as bell ringing, an apparently spontaneous pealing of bells. A rare manuscript called *Bealings' Bells* was published in 1841 by a Major Edward Moore, F.R.S. This work describes cases of bell-ringing, including an incident in which bells rang spontaneously for fifty-three consecutive days in the town of Great Bealings, Suffolk, England.

In 1868, an American publication, the *Atlantic Monthly,* carried a story about a bell-ringing incident, which included other poltergeist activity. This activity centered around an Irish servant girl named Mary Carrick. Shortly after she began working for an American family, all the bells in the house would ring spontaneously every half hour. The family ordered the wires to be detached from the bells, but the ringing continued.

In addition to the ringing, a loud rapping and knocking was heard frequently throughout the house. Moving objects would follow the girl as she did her work. On one occasion, an ironing board and a nearby table rose into the air while she was ironing. Another time, a heavy stone slab lifted itself as lightly as a feather.

Bewildered and upset by these unusual occurrences, Mary Carrick lost her reason and entered an insane asylum.

A bell-ringing incident is one of the many legends surrounding Padre Serra, an early California missionary and ascetic of the eighteenth century. When he died, bells were heard to ring spontaneously at Monterey, the place of his death. Residents of the area claimed that the bells had been rung by the hands of angels.

Rock Throwing

In 1964, an incident occurred in the Philippine Islands that was sufficiently dramatic to be written up in the newspapers and to draw large crowds of incredulous spectators.

A homeless fourteen-year-old boy was offered a home by a kindly family living in a small village. After the boy's arrival, the family found their home frequently bombarded by rocks. The father of the family blamed the neighbors and reported the episode to the police. However, a thorough investigation showed no evidence which could link the neighbors to the rock throwing.

A civic leader of the town, hearing of the circumstances, suggested moving the boy to her home. As soon as he moved in, her house became the target of the rock throwing. She noted that the boy was always asleep when the rocks were thrown; therefore, he could not have been responsible for causing the bombardment. Many people watched the house day and night, but were unable to find anyone who could be suspected of causing the assault.

The child was next sent to live with a relative, but the stoning followed him and continued for ten days at the relative's home. This particular house was beside a river, and it was believed that the rocks must have come from the river bed, but an examination of them showed them to be quite dry and unlike the rocks found in the river bed.

After being placed in still another home with no better results, the youth was taken in by Father Salas, the local parish priest. The rectory was struck heavily, smashing some of the windows. On one occasion, more than one hundred rocks were collected during a period of two and one half hours. Crowds gathered to witness this spectacle. After exorcising his church, the priest brought the child to a Boy's Town in a nearby city. The case was no longer mentioned in the news and psychic researchers interested in the case were unable to obtain further information.

The Miami Poltergeist

One of the most intensively researched and well-publicized cases of the twentieth century took place in 1967 in Miami, Florida. This case was so unusual that a special symposium entitled "The Miami Poltergeist" was held at the annual convention of the Parapsychological Association in New York in September, 1967. Such noted researchers as Dr. J. Gaither Pratt of the University of Virginia and W.G. Roll of the Psychical Research Foundation of Durham, North Carolina, studied the case thoroughly and stated publicly that they found no evidence indicating trickery. A varied group of policemen, researchers, media reporters, magicians, and ministers were present during many of the startling events, and all agreed that there was no possibility of fraud.

The center of all this excitement was a nineteen-year-old boy named Julio. At the beginning of these dramatic events, Julio was a shipping clerk in the warehouse of a Miami gift company. While he was working at the warehouse, strange accidents began happening. Cartons would tip over, spilling their contents on the floor. Glass objects would spontaneously burst, and soon ashtrays were flying on a curve across the room.

At first, this activity was not connected with Julio, who was as surprised and frightened by it as everyone else. When the connection was made, investigators were soon invading the warehouse with cameras which followed Julio's every move. A thorough search was made for threads or wires that Julio might be using to move these articles around as a giant hoax. No threads or wires were found, and the constant observation of Julio showed that he could have had no opportunity to deliberately cause the disturbances.

After his fear had subsided, Julio began to enjoy the attention and publicity which he was accorded. Soon, however, the amazing events became serious.

One night, a mysterious robbery occurred in the warehouse. In the morning, the managers found the burglar alarm torn out by the roots and little piles of burned newspaper on the floor. A few items and some petty cash were missing from a cabinet which had been locked. The key which evidently had been used to open the cabinet had been returned to its proper place. Julio's car had been seen nearby that night by neighbors, and Julio became the obvious suspect. Julio himself claimed to have no recollection of the events of that night.

After the robbery and the subsequent police investigation, a controversy arose on the subject of Julio's poltergeist. The newspapers claimed that the poltergeist activity had all been a hoax played with threads and vibrations. The investigators who had been present during the activity remained convinced that Julio could not have deliberately been the cause. Examination by a psychiatrist showed that the boy was not emotionally disturbed except for the confusion which had been caused in his mind by the unwieldy powers and the reactions of others to it. The psychiatrist also believed that a repressed hostility toward his father was causing Julio to direct his powers against his employers.

W.G. Roll was highly interested in the case and brought Julio to the Institute of Parapsychology in Durham, North Carolina, to be studied under laboratory conditions. The tests for psychokinesis, or PK, are conducted with dice machines. The subject attempts to influence the number which will appear on the dice. All of the tests done on Julio for PK were positive.

Julio returned to Miami, where he found a new job in a shoe store. Shortly after he started to work, objects in the store became activated. A heavy fire extinguisher, firmly anchored to its base, suddenly crashed onto the floor. Shot glasses exploded or fell off shelves. Bottles of shoe polish flew across the room, sometimes around corners. During all of these "accidents," Julio was visible to the other employees.

The boss agreed not to fire Julio on account of the poltergeist, but working conditions became extremely difficult. The poltergeist activity was heaviest on the days when Julio was upset or angry.

Eventually Julio was fired for the more mundane fault of rudeness to a customer. After he left, the boss's wife remembered the one incident that had made her most uneasy about the young stock clerk. He had come to work one day with a swollen eye and she had inquired about it. He had given her a strange look, and the next day her eye was swollen in the same manner.

After leaving the shoe store, Julio found a job as a stock boy in the Kress Store. Again, upon his arrival, objects began flying and bottles exploding. Cups disintegrated into tiny fragments. On many of these occasions, other employees swore that Julio had been standing beside them as they watched the objects careen around the room.

Eventually, Julio left his job and married his boyhood sweetheart. He went to work at a service station, where he was shot while trying to prevent a robbery. The Psychical Research Foundation remained interested in him, but he was unwilling to be a guinea pig for their experiments.

His unconscious psychokinetic ability seemed to diminish slightly as he grew older, but his wife has reason to be wary. One evening, going into the kitchen after a quarrel with Julio, she narrowly missed being hit by an exploding shot glass.

The poltergeist has come a long way over the centuries. No longer a fearsome demon, it has become known as a product of supernatural ability possessed by unusual individuals. In the future of psychokinesis, one can envision the harnessing of the poltergeist in the laboratory, possibly to be channeled into ways that would benefit mankind.

11. Tennessee's Famous Bell Witch

The Nature of the Bell Witch

IN THE COUNTY OF Robertson, Tennessee, touching the state line of Kentucky, is a small community called Adam. Adam is the site of the famous Bell Witch, the most puzzling of all occult personalities south of the Mason-Dixon line.

In 1817, this phenomenon made its manifestations, first as a disembodied voice and a night prankster, later as a strong, playful, mischievous or malevolent force. The many biographers of the Bell Witch have never agreed whether to call this strange being a witch, a ghost, or a poltergeist. John Bell, who was tormented and driven to an early grave by the Bell Witch, spoke of it (or her) as "the Spirit." Mrs. Bell called this callous interloper, this disturber of their home "the Trouble."

When John Bell asked the witch who she was, she told him to call her "Kate."

There was a woman in the community named Kate Batts, a widow who was forthright, outspoken, and solid of frame. She was odd, but she was not evil. On the contrary, she was very moraland very honest, and had no known connection with Kate, the Bell Witch.

John Bell never clearly understood why the spirit wanted to be called Kate. Many persons thought that the witch used this name in order to hide her real identity.

In many ways the Bell Witch resembled a poltergeist who would assault the Bell family, pulling their hair viciously or tangling and knotting it. The victim's cheek would be slapped sharply or the bed covers tugged off. As in many poltergeist cases, the earliest manifestations of the personality were in the form of door bangings and rappings. However, these were accompanied by a disembodied voice, and later by many appearances in a visible form, which are not characteristic of the poltergeist. At times, Kate did not appear, but she left tangible signs of her presence. On one occasion she left a dead rat on a snow-white bed to prove she had threatened a member of the Bell family.

The Bell Witch seemed to know about things that were hidden to others. Often she located stolen horses for the Bells' neighbors. She would inform the owner of a stolen horse where his animal was being held, and the owner would always find his horse as she advised. The witch could, and did, carry bits of information from house to house. Her main center, however, was the Bell home.

The most mistreated victims of the Bell Witch were John Bell, the wealthy planter, and his daughter Betsy. It seemed, in fact, that these two were the prime targets of the Bell Witch's attack on the unfortunate family.

The Bell family was concerned that "their trouble" should receive no publicity. However, as the acts of the witch became more and more harmful and disturbing, the minister, the school teacher, and certain friends were begged to come to the house to try to help the Bells get rid of the Witch. At one point a British gentleman who called himself a successful exorcist tried to vanquish it.

During the third year of the witch's activities, several neighbors were invited to the Bell home to witness its pranks and to join the Bells in an earnest request that it leave them alone. These were friends and acquaintances from nearby farms, some of whom had experienced the antics of the Bell Witch. But always, the Bell family implored that the matter be kept as quiet as possible because they were not only puzzled but ashamed of the whole thing.

The Voice of the Bell Witch

The voice of the witch was most often shrill, metallic, and punctuated with the crackling laugh and derisive chuckle usually associated with witches. Strangely, however, the voice of Kate could also be gentle and persuasive.

An unusual characteristic of the Bell Witch was her ability to repeat perfectly the prayers and whole sermons of both the community ministers. It became a regular event for people to gather in the Bell home on Sunday evenings to witness, or hear, Kate.

Someone would ask Kate aloud, "What was Brother Sugg's text?" The answer would come back immediately. Sometimes certain points of theology would be brought up for argument. Kate could quote additional passages to prove a certain point, usually convincing all present of her stupendous knowledge of both the Old and New Testaments.

On one occasion she gave the sermons of Brother Sugg Fort, who had preached at Drakes Pond Methodist Church, and of Reverend James Gunn, who had preached at Bethel Methodist Church that same morning at 11:00. The assemblage asked how the witch knew these sermons, both of which had been delivered some twenty miles apart at the same hour. The answer was, "I know because I was there."

At times Kate would appear to be religious, while at others she was abusive of religion. She often shrieked out vicious condemnations, revilings, cursings and blasphemies.

The Appearances of the Witch

Besides speaking aloud, the witch was able to manifest itself in a variety of physical forms. The persons who saw the Bell Witch most often were John Bell, Betsy Bell, and Dean, a slave, who was also the trusted friend of John Bell.

Many of the witch's manifestations were in the form of animals. The witch appeared several times to Dean and the Bell sons as a large dog with flaming yellow-green eyes and a forked tail resembling that of a dinosaur or the Devil. The dog would appear and disappear at will. At times the witch would appear as a very large bird, larger than a turkey. At other times it would appear as a small bird perched on a fence.

Once the Bell Witch appeared to Betsy as a huge talking fish which warned her to give up her betrothal to Josh Gardner. Kate also appeared once as a large rabbit. The rabbit form was seen by a Mr. Johnson and a son of the family as the two men were riding their horses. That same evening, Kate told the family of her rabbit appearance.

The witch could also take on human form. Fantastically, she could appear as a most delicate, long haired, green-eyed little female child, always dressed in green. This form of Kate was seen by Betsy, her sister, and her girl friends.

Kate once also appeared to Betsy in the form of an old woman. Betsy had led a group of children to the woods to gather flowers for the church and was in the joyous act of breaking off a branch of white dogwood blossoms, when she heard the familiar voice of Kate telling her not to dare to break the branch. When she looked up, she saw a very wrinkled, very thin old woman with red-rimmed eyes hanging by her arms from a nearby tree. Betsy did not pick the flowers, but immediately took the children in her care out of the woodland, not explaining the reason for the sudden change of plans.

On one occasion the Bell Witch appeared as a multiple personality. Betsy, her sister, and several of their friends were walking down the road toward their home. On a rail fence sat a group of people: a little girl in green, a woman resembling a person in the community named Mrs. Kate Batts, and several round-faced children. The voice of the Bell Witch said: "This is my family." Some of the young men in the group shot at these strange apparitions. The strange images hid behind some fallen logs nearby and jeered at Betsy's friends, then disappeared.

The Attack on Betsy Bell

Elizabeth Bell was the youngest of the Bell children. A fair and pretty girl, she was the pet of the family, but was not spoiled. At school she met Josh Gardner, a neighbor's son. The two became sweethearts, and everyone believed that they would be married. Before the engagement, however, the witch told the girl she would not allow this marriage. Betsy disregarded the warning, and the witch began to torment her.

The witch visited Betsy often at night pulling her hair and slapping her cheeks. Once, Kate struck Betsy's face hard enough to leave long red marks.

On one occasion, Betsy had asked her mother for a new dress to wear to a corn-shucking at which Josh would be present. At this public gathering, Kate spoke aloud so that all could hear. She shamed the young girl for getting a new dress to tempt the Gardner boy. Betsy left the party in tears.

Shortly after Josh had given Betsy an engagement ring, the couple went to a fishing party on the Red River. On this occasion it was said that Kate appeared as the largest fish anyone had ever seen. Several men tried to get hold of the fish after it had been hooked. It was unlike any of the native fish in appearance; it defied the men, shook them off, and swam upstream. After wresting itself from the sturdy men, the fish said aloud: "Please Betsy, don't have Josh Gardner!" Betsy broke her engagement that day.

The witch sometimes put a fainting spell on Betsy. Each evening at a certain hour, Betsy would have trouble breathing. For thirty or forty minutes she would be unconscious. During this time, the witch never spoke aloud. As soon as Betsy regained consciousness, the witch would start talking to the whole household. These tactics convinced Betsy more than ever that she should heed the witch's warning not to marry Josh Gardner.

Betsy later married another man and Josh moved away from the community because Betsy feared that he might fall prey to Kate as had her father. In a neighboring County, Obion, there is a site called Gardner Station, named for this eighteen-year-old suitor of Betsy Bell.

The harassments of Betsy by the witch continued to be so multitudinous and cruel that the family sent Betsy to stay with friends several miles distant, so that Mr. Bell, who was being tortured to death, could not see his beloved child suffer.

"Kate" and Mrs. Bell

Strangely enough, the witch seemed to respect and like Mrs. Bell and never harassed her in her sleep as she did to the rest of the family. She would speak aloud to her, offering her advice and comfort when she was ill. At one time, she broke some nuts with which Mrs. Bell was having difficulty and dropped the shells and nuts into Mrs. Bell's apron. On another occasion Kate offered bunches of fresh grapes to her when she had been ill. The witch did not appear, but the grapes were tangible enough to be tasted by several people who were visiting Mrs. Bell.

The Death of John Bell

The witch had told John Bell that she meant to take his

life and that she would certainly be the cause of his early death. As time went on, Mr. Bell began to suffer from a strange malady. He described the feeling in his mouth and throat as "like a stick having been placed to block both speech and eating." It was as if his mouth, tongue, and throat were paralyzed. The attack would leave him, then return. After continued attacks Mr. Bell's tongue became swollen. His face muscles would twitch and contort.

The diary of Mr. Bell's son Richard William Bell, *Our Family Trouble*, describes the terrible plight of the wealthy planter:

> After being tormented almost beyond human endurance, father had grown so miserable that he never walked alone about the premises. Early one morning during the summer of 1820, he requested me to go with him to his hog pen several hundred yards from the house. He wished to direct the hands in separating the porkers from the stock hogs.
>
> We had gone but a short distance from the house when one of his shoes was jerked from his foot. I replaced it, tying a double bow knot. A few steps further on . . . the other shoe was jerked off.
>
> The account continues that on the way back to the house both shoes were again jerked off Mr. Bell and he was struck across the face so forcibly that he fell across a log. Mr. Bell finally exclaimed:
>
> "Oh, my dear son, I cannot longer stand the persecutions of this terrible thing. It is killing me; I feel that the end is near, and I will welcome the day."

Mr. Bell asked that his son not tell of this episode, and the secret was kept. The diary goes on to tell that Mr. Bell prayed that God in His wisdom would release him from the power of this demon.

John Bell took to his bed in October, 1820. He grew steadily worse. Different doctors were summoned, but none could name the illness nor cure him. On December 20 Mr. Bell seemed very near death. The doctor and close friends were summoned to the bedside. On this occasion it was discovered that a green bottle of medicine given by the doctor to reduce the pain had disappeared, but a small black vial had been set on the shelf in the same spot. The doctor sniffed the liquid in the bottle and confirmed that the breath of the dying John Bell had the same odor. Mrs. Bell had not seen this new medication and had been unable to get her husband to swallow anything or, in fact, to rouse him from his coma.

The doctor and friends decided to test this strange liquid, which they suspected to be a type of poison. They drew a broom straw into the vial, then across the tongue of a cat. The cat went immediately into convulsions and died on the floor of the bedroom.

John Bell died on December 21, 1820. As his body was lowered into the grave, the voice of "Kate" was heard. It was loud, derisive, and gleeful as it sang the old drinking song, "Row Me Up Some Brandy, O!"

Andrew Jackson and the Bell Witch

It is on record that John Bell and Andrew Jackson were good friends. Eight years before Jackson became president, Mr. Bell sent for Jackson to help him discover the strengths of the witch and to help release his family from the terrorizing powers of "the spirit."

According to the historian Colonel Thomas Yancey: "General Jackson and his men were riding on horseback discussing how they were going to do up the witch . . . when just within a short distance of the (Bell) house, traveling over a smooth, level piece of road the (party's supply) wagon halted and stuck fast . . . as if welded to the earth."

A member of the party recounted, "A sharp, metallic voice came from the bushes, saying, 'All right, General, I'll let the wagon move on.' "

Jackson exclaimed, "By the Eternal, boys, it's the witch. This is worse than fighting the British!"

The wagon was freed and Jackson continued on to the Bell farm house, where he spent two unsuccessful days trying to find an explanation for the mysterious goings-on before returning to Nashville.

On U.S. Highway 41, near the spot where Jackson's wagon was halted, there is today a marker which reads, in part, "The witch scared off Betsy Bell's suitor . . . No satisfactory explanation of the witch has ever been advanced."

Threats of the Bell Witch

The Bell Witch appeared in 1817, stayed four terrifying

years, through the death of John Bell, went away for seven years, then returned for a visit. At this time it was repeated that the "Spirit" would return 107 years after the first visit in 1817.

When Dr. Charles Bailey Bell decided to write about the witch using the guarded family diary, it was close to 107 years after the first manifestation of the witch. Dr. Bell stated that events were occurring just as had been threatened and these were some of the reasons for his preparing the exposé.

Still later, Robert Borden Adam, son of Ann Bell Adam, the daughter of John Elijah Bell II, made these admissions of the realization of the witch's vicious threats:

His grandmother, the widow of John Elijah Bell II, died in the same way as the original John Bell, with stiffness in the mouth and the inability to speak.

Ann Bell Adam was a member of the generation living in 1935 and was therefore meant to receive the curse.

In 1968, her husband and two daughters were killed in a fire which had mysteriously started in their house.

On May 5 of that year, Ann Bell Adam called a friend and said, "I've taken sleeping tablets."

The friend said, "Good. You need a long night's sleep."

She replied, "I've taken 78 of them." She died in spite of attempts to rescue her.

Her son, Robert Borden Adam, is sure that the Bell Witch was responsible for her death.

By sheer coincidence, he married a girl named Betsy.

The wild, provoking stories of the Bell Witch are still told today in and around Nashville. Most grandmothers have told their sons and daughters of events concerning the Bell Witch that occurred in the days of their parents. Today she is often the main spirit invoked at séances performed at slumber parties. No one has yet discovered who or what the Bell Witch really is, or whether she might someday return to strike new victims.

12. Ghost Appearances

Ghosts and Kings

MANY TALES are told of the dealings of heads of state with the supernatural. Certain countries of Europe even had their own "personal ghosts," who seemed determined to guide the nation's leaders. These spirits include the White Lady of the Hohenzollerns of Prussia, the Little Man in Grey of Sweden, and the Red Man of France.

The White Lady of the Hohenzollerns was a white, shadowy figure who could be seen floating through the gardens of the Royal Palace shortly before the death of any member of the royal family. If she wore black gloves, a man would die; if she wore white gloves, a woman would die. One of her appearances concerns King Frederick William I, father of Frederick the Great, who had two coffins made for himself and his queen. One night, the king forced his wife to lie in her coffin, implying that he thought her death was near. When the White Lady passed through the garden later that night, the queen's death seemed certain, until someone noticed that she was wearing black gloves, and therefore it was the king who was to die.

The Little Man in Grey was a ghostly adviser to many Swedish monarchs. He would appear only before royalty to deliver his grim messages. King Charles XII of Sweden went to find the Little Man in Grey in the hope that the spirit could give him some inspiration on how to guide his life, which seemed unsatisfactory. In response to the king's ritual chant, the spirit appeared in the form of an icy figure. His message was not heartening. The Little Man in Grey chastised King Charles for his failure to bring Christianity to Turkey and for putting his vanity before the welfare of his country. He predicted that the king's soul would return to earth three times more as a soldier-king who would endanger his country by his greed. Before vanishing, he gave Charles a ring, as cold as a circle of ice, which he said would vanish on the day of the king's death.

The Red Man of France, who appeared to Napoleon as he had to other rulers of the country, came to the Emperor to forewarn him of disaster. Appearing to Napoleon on three occasions as a tall man in a red costume, the spirit warned the monarch that if he persisted in attempting to conquer all of Europe, he would be doomed. The undaunted little warrior paid no heed to the warning. The outcome is history.

Lincoln's Ghost

Some ghosts are nameless, and some are dearly familiar to those who had been close to them in life; but the ghost who appeared to a man named Carl Schurz would be familiar to anyone. He was the ghost of Abraham Lincoln.

Schurz was a notable German-American statesman who was active during Lincoln's administration. After Lincoln's death, Schurz was living in Wisconsin when he was summoned to Washington by President Andrew Johnson. Before reaching Washington, he made a stopover in Philadelphia to visit some friends, the Tiedemanns. Their daughter had developed mediumistic powers, and it was suggested that a séance be held that evening.

After contacting the spirit of Schiller, who identified himself by writing a line of verse in German, Mr. Schurz asked the medium to contact Abraham Lincoln.

When the medium announced Lincoln's presence, Mr. Schurz asked if he could tell him anything about President Johnson's purpose in summoning him to Washington. Lincoln's reply was that the president wished Schurz to undertake a journey. The spirit surprised Schurz by adding that Schurz would one day become a senator of the United States from Missouri. Since he was a resident of Wisconsin and had no thought of becoming a senator at all, he was mystified by this prediction.

However, two years later, an unexpected business proposition took Schurz to Missouri and in 1869, he was elected to the United States Senate by the Legislature of Missouri. As for the journey undertaken for the president, Johnson did indeed send Schurz on a trip through the South to study conditions in those states. The ghost of Abraham Lincoln had spoken the truth.

The Haunted Dakota Apartments

The upper West Side of New York City has many old, strange-looking houses that seem as though they might easily be haunted. Many of them are. One of these is the Dakota Apartments, which faces Central Park.

The Dakota would stand out under any circumstances. Built at a time when upper Manhattan was still partly rural, it was named the "Dakota" because it was so far away from everything that "it might as well as be in the Dakota Territory." It stands unchanged today, a massive, square stone structure built around a courtyard.

The Dakota first achieved notoriety when it was used as the setting for the chilling movie about witches and devils *Rosemary's Baby*. New Yorkers who had never known much about the building became fascinated with its forbidding air.

Susy Smith tells a story of a recent ghost in the Dakota Apartments in *Ghosts around the House*:

Television producer Gary Smith was apparently not put off by the possibility of ghosts when he decided to move his family into the Dakota, in the apartment formerly occupied by singer Judy Holliday.

The apartment was decorated in a gloomy manner. Everything was either painted grey or black or paneled with dark wood. Mr. Smith hired three young men to refinish the apartment before he moved in with his family.

The young men, two of whom were particularly interested in the occult, felt the presence of a ghost shortly after they had begun their work. One night, one of these boys brought an Ouija Board into the apartment. They asked the Ouija "spirit" if there was indeed a ghost present. It answered in the affirmative and added that the ghost resented their attempts to paint the bedroom which had been his. The ghostgave his name, but unfortunately the young men forgot it, so they were unable to verify whether or not such a person had actually lived in the apartment.

Later, two of the boys saw the ghost materialize. The first one to see it was busy painting when he became aware of someone watching him. Turning, he saw the transparent figure of a boy about nine or ten years old. The child was dressed in the type of short pants, jacket, and vest that small boys wore at about the turn of the century. The ghost watched the young man work for a while, then he wandered away toward one of the bedrooms.

The second young man saw the ghost as a young man in his twenties. This apparition was tall, but his face was as childish as that of the smaller ghost. The observer received the impression that the youth was retarded. This spirit was dressed, like the child ghost, in the formal manner of an earlier era. He was wearing a smoking jacket with an oversized floppy bow tie.

The two young men felt that both these ghosts had been manifestations of the same spirit at different points in his lifetime. Both felt that the ghost was attempting to prevent them from changing the surroundings which had become familiar to him. This feeling was reinforced by something which happened to one of them.

He was painting the large walk-in closet when the door suddenly closed and the light went off. Turning the light back on, he propped the door open and continued working. After a few moments, his hand suddenly froze in midair. He felt it being forced down against the bare light bulb and held there long enough to be painfully burned.

As he recalled the incident afterward, he says that he then "did some magic" which he knew and the ghost apparently went away. It was not seen or heard for several weeks. Later, it reappeared, but attempted no further harm.

After the Smith family moved into the apartment, the ghost seemed to be gone for good. One day, however, two of the young men came back to complete some work, and each sensed the presence of the ghost in the house again. Without telling one another, each traced the ghost to the bedroom which the spirit claimed was formerly his. When they compared their conclusions, they both agreed that they had sensed a human presence inside the large stuffed dog which belonged to the Smith children. One of them had seen an aura around the toy and they both noticed the strangely musty odor which they had sensed on the ghost. When they later noticed the children playing with the dog,

Mrs. Smith remarked that the dog had never particularly interested the children until they had moved to the Dakota. It was as if the presence of the childlike ghost had made the stuffed animal a more attractive playmate.

Much later, one of the young men saw the ghost walking slowly away with his back held straight in a somber manner. He felt that this time the spirit was departing for good. Looking around the apartment, he saw that the large stuffed dog had disappeared from the Smith household, undoubtedly leaving the playful spirit no suitable place to inhabit.

PART IV

13. The Invisible Population of India

Ghosts of Home and Countryside

INDIA IS A COUNTRY which is crowded not only with people, but with ghosts and spirits. The ghosts of India are not frightening white-sheeted figures, but vibrant personalities, as often benevolent as evil. They inspire awe rather than terror.

In a land which has become known as a mecca of faith and spiritual growth, and where belief in reincarnation and miracles is standard, it is not surprising that so many of its people claim to have a personal knowledge of ghosts. Some of these ghosts are said to live under spreading bushes with spade-shaped leaves, known as *pipul* bushes. Others inhabit homes alongside living people, and their presence is felt throughout the house.

It is believed that anyone who can capture a ghost is very fortunate; for the ghost, like the legendary genie of the lamp, becomes a servant when captured and must grant his captor whatever he wishes. There is an interesting aspect to the ghost's service; if the master requests food to be brought from outside, he must give the ghost money with which to purchase the food, for a ghost will never permit himself to steal.

To capture a ghost is not a simple matter of luck. A person desiring to capture a ghost must be spiritually advanced and must know the special ritual. If the ritual, which is of a religious nature, is not performed properly, the captured ghost can become malevolent and turn against his captor, causing bad luck to follow him.

Possession by Ghosts

Malevolent ghosts have been said to enter into a person's

body in a way similar to the alleged possession by the Devil. In one such case, a young woman was given milk on her wedding night by an envious servant who had placed cremation ashes in it. These ashes were believed to still contain the ghost of the deceased. After that night, the bride was stricken by a mysterious disease resembling epilepsy. She was injured in several accidents in which others escaped unharmed. Her family and friends believed that the ghost had taken over her body and intended to slowly destroy it. Her body became battered from falls and self-inflicted wounds, while her mind clouded so that she could not even recognize her own children. Her condition deteriorated in spite of attempts at medical treatment, and she died when she was barely forty years old.

It has been demonstrated in India that those who are believed to be possessed by ghosts acquire extraordinary powers of insight during the times that the ghost is inside the body. People learn which residents of their area are possessed and can recognize the periods in which the ghost is active. At these times, the possessed individual is approached by people in the street who wish to know their future. The one who is possessed will produce statements which contain enough truth to amaze his listeners. Thus, these tormented people become the oracles of the community. The unusual physical strength which they display contributes to their reputation of power.

As in the medieval Christian tradition, exorcism is the only cure for possession. The exorcism is performed by the astrologer, who is the seat of magical knowledge in the community. As the ghost is released from the body, the victim undergoes contortions and convulsions, then relaxes and remains at peace. Although exorcisms are performed regularly among the Hindus, many families will not submit a possessed relative to this ritual for fear that an improperly performed exorcism may worsen the victim's condition.

The Ghostly Wedding Party

One of the older stories of a man's encounter with spirits concerns a man who was crossing the jungle one evening and came upon a wedding party dancing and singing. He was invited to join the group and spent several hours celebrating with them. As he took leave of the party, some of the members of the group filled a bag with food from the celebration for the unexpected guest to take home with him. On arriving at home, he opened the bag and found a collection of stones. He knew then that the people whom he had seen had not been human, but ghosts. The food and drink had no substance, for ghosts have no need of nourishment.

The Ghost Who Reappeared in a Dream

Much more recently, a New Delhi youth was sought out by a ghost for no apparent reason, then revisited in a dream more than ten years later.

The boy, Jinder, the son of a wealthy businessman, was in his home one day when he heard the doorbell ring. He was accustomed to having the servants answer the door, but on that day the house was strangely silent and the bell continued to ring. His grandmother came to him and suggested, perhaps with some intuitive knowledge, that he should answer the door himself. Reluctantly, Jinder opened the door to find a young man whom he had never seen before.

The stranger asked to speak to the boy privately, but when Jinder invited him into the house, he refused. Instead, he suggested that they should go to some public place to talk. Jinder was wary about going outside with the stranger. It was almost noon, the time when the people of India prefer to be indoors, for it is believed that the spirits walk outside in the noon hour. Also, Jinder had been involved in fights with other boys and had reason to fear that this stranger might be a messenger of revenge. However, he was curious and did not want to admit to fear. He decided to go with the stranger after telling his brothers to come after him if he did not return in two hours.

Jinder and the stranger walked together to the chosen meetingplace, a small café in the neighborhood. During the walk, they did not speak to one another. In the restaurant, the stranger remained silent while Jinder ordered two cups of coffee.

The coffee was brought, and still the stranger did not speak. Jinder grew more uneasy, but he was hesitant to open a conversation wich might lead in some unknown and terrible direction. The stranger seemed satisfied merely to study Jinder's features as if drawing some information from them.

Suddenly Jinder looked up from his coffee. Out of the corner of his eye it had seemed that something in the room had changed. The stranger had gone, his cup of coffee still untouched on the table.

It took only a brief glance around the room for Jinder to see that the stranger was no longer in the café. It hardly seemed possible that the man could have left so hurriedly without making a sound. Calling the waiter, Jinder asked him if he had seen the other gentleman leave.

"What other gentleman?" asked the waiter. "You came alone, sir. I wondered why you ordered two cups of coffee for yourself."

Although he could never truly understand the full meaning of that strange meeting, Jinder felt that a ghost had come to him with some message, but had found him unprepared at that time.

Many years later, in America, Jinder had a dream of a stranger leading him on a mysterious journey. Traveling in a car, the two men passed through several barriers which appeared impassable. Leaving a bumpy, rutted road surrounded by barren country, they entered a smooth road leading through a luxuriant countryside. Jinder wanted to linger at this stage of the journey, but the stranger urged him to continue further. The final barrier was so intricate that it was impossible for the car to pass through.

"We will not need the car any longer," said the stranger, and the two men went through on foot. They were now in a peaceful land with roads leading in many directions. Jinder awoke, knowing that the dream was complete.

The dream is similar to the classic journey toward spiritual advancement which is found in the literature of many cultures. After having this dream interpreted by a psychic to mean that he would have a period of material prosperity which he would cast aside in order to grow spiritually (symbolized by the abandoning of the car), Jinder recalled the meeting with the vanishing stranger so many years before. It seemed to him that the stranger had been a benevolent ghost coming to bring him spiritual knowledge, but had found the boy too involved with himself and with the material world. Later, the same ghost had come to Jinder the man and had found him in his maturity more ready to look ahead toward a time when he could become more spiritually aware. Possibly because Jinder had left India, it was necessary for the ghost to speak to him through a dream rather than to appear in the shape of a living man. Even a ghost might be limited by a geographic boundary or by a hesitancy to enter a country less sympathetic to the spirit world.

Astrologers

An astrologer is a very respected figure in a Hindu community. Most families have a personal astrologer, who charts the horoscope of each family member from the moment of birth. At decisive moments in a person's life, the astrologer is consulted for guidance. When marriages are arranged by the parents, as is the custom in India, the astrologer is called in to determine if the charts of the future bride and groom predict compatibility. The word of the astrologer is highly regarded; few parents would risk arranging an ill-starred marriage.

When an astrologer comes to a home for consultation, he asks each member of the family to bring him an item within a specific category; for example, a fruit or a flower. If he guesses beforehand which type of fruit or flower will be brought by the individual, then he is attuned to this person at the time and will have an interesting message for him.

Charting horoscopes is not the sole function of the Hindu astrologer. Although he is on a higher intellectual level than the witch doctors of the more primitive cultures, he too fills the role of all-purpose wise man. Many Hindus consult the astrologer for a cure before consulting the doctor.

The ancient magic circle, bordered with cabalistic symbols, is used by the Hindu astrologer as a protection for those whom he is attempting to cure. Spells and holy water from the Ganges are also part of his magic.

When a child suffers from nightmares, his parents may bring him to the family astrologer. The man will sprinkle the child with holy water, circle him, and murmur some words in Sanskrit. From that time, the child's dreams will be peaceful. Hindus who today are grown and educated can remember the power of the astrologer who was able to free them from their night terrors.

An astrologer can also help a person to fulfill a wish. A man came to his astrologer asking for a way to ensure that his son, whom he had not seen in many years, would return home soon for a visit. The astrologer advised the man to wear a cap for the next three months. He did so, and within that time the son returned, more surprised than the father.

The astrologer is rarely asked for love charms or philtres, since marriages are almost always arranged by parents. Hindus are more likely to ask for charms of a practical nature—to aid in business or in passing exams.

Astrology is a family business in India. The trade, with its store of knowledge, is passed from father to son through many generations.

Hindu Superstitions and Taboos

The Hindus, like the people of most ancient cultures, have certain superstitions and taboos which have been handed down through the generations. There are few people of India who have not at some time found at least a few of these beliefs influencing their daily lives.

If a person sneezes once, he is unlucky that day and should stay home. If he sneezes twice, his luck is good and he may go out confidently.

To win a case in court, a man should carry a piece of clothing which was worn by his child when it was newborn.

If a man wishes for something, he makes a promise that he will fast every Tuesday if his wish is granted. He must not ask for material fulfillment, but for a less tangible goal.

Certain superstitions exist concerning death. The Hindus, who cremate their dead, are especially fearful of graveyards, which are used in India mainly by Moslems and Christians.

It is bad luck to jump or step over a tombstone. However, if the coffin of an old man is being carried through the cemetery, anyone who passes under it will live for as many years as the deceased lived.

A person who dies in bed will be unhappy in his next life.

A dying person is therefore placed on the floor.

Cats are bad omens and are generally disliked in India. It is considered unlucky to see a cat early in the morning.

Red is a magic color and is used in spells. A married woman must make a red mark every day on her scalp to identify her marital status. It is believed that if a woman forgets to make this mark, her husband will die.

It is unlucky to go into the street at noon, for the spirits are known to walk about at this hour.

Anyone who looks in the mirror at night is likely to have bad dreams.

Dreams which occur after four o'clock in the morning are known to come true.

When Hindus bathe in the natural mineral spring, they must throw money into the water as payment for its beneficial effects.

Earthquakes are frequent in India. If anyone has the presence of mind to eat a bit of dust from the ground during an earthquake, he will be protected against disease.

Since children are extremely important and much loved in India, certain superstitions and practices are concerned with the protection of children.

When a child becomes three years old, he is brought to a temple to have his head shaved. During the journey from home to the temple, the family must not stop or the child will be injured in an accident.

Children must be protected from the evil eye of *tonas*, who are witch-like old women. To protect a child, the parents make a black mark on its body. This mark is also said to prevent colic.

If the child is already cursed with the evil eye, its parents take the long, hot green peppers known as finger peppers, circle them seven times over the child's head, and then burn them in the fire.

Little girls are considered to be "lakshmi," or wealth. Anyone who kicks a little girl will become impoverished mentally, physically, and financially.

Fakirs

The *fakirs*, or magicians, of India have a repertoire of dramatic and daring feats. They lie on beds of nails, walk through fire, pass swords through their throats, and, if the fakir is especially skillful, perform the Indian rope trick.

Investigation of the fakirs has shown that their stunts are actually magicians' tricks and have little or nothing to do with occult power. In some cases, the fakir has studied *yoga*, the discipline of control over mind and body. This control helps him to voluntarily anesthetize his body against pain.

Most of the tricks, such as walking through flames or lying on nails, are easily duplicated by competent magicians and have even been performed by amateurs. Psychic investigator and author Raymond Bayless claims to have duplicated many of the fakir's tricks. Mr. Bayless also observed the performance of a fakir who was able to pass a sword through his throat. The feat was made possible by the two holes which the performer had pierced through his throat in the same manner that earlobes are pierced for earrings.

A more skillful type of Eastern magician makes use of subtle hypnotism. One successful performer would arrive at ten minutes to nine for a performance scheduled for six o'clock. After quieting the complaining audience, he would instruct them to look at their watches. Every watch would appear to say 5:59. At nine o'clock he would awaken the audience and the people would leave believing that they had witnessed a three-hour performance.

The Indian rope trick is possibly performed with this type of hypnotism. In this famous stunt, a fakir makes a rope rise from the ground. A young boy climbs up the rope and disappears into the sky. This trick has mystified scores of audiences. Many witnesses claimed to have taken a picture of the rope trick; when the film was developed, the pictures would be blank.

Although there may not be a truly occult explanation of the Indian rope trick, its performance remains a colorful mystery of Eastern showmanship.

It seems likely that India is the original birthplace of the awareness of ghosts and spirit forms. The English, who spent so many years in India, are often in tune with ideas concerning the supernatural and have produced many famous psychics and astrologers who have spread their talents through the Western world.

Beginning with the spiritualist revival of the late

nineteenth century, India's spiritual influence gradually was felt in the United States. Ghosts have been heard from in this country manytimes over the years. Some have been evil ghosts, intent on causing terror and destruction in the homes which they have invaded. Others have been spirits of peace, coming to enlighten and protect those whom they touch. Although it will be a long time before these beings from another sphere can gain the acceptance they have so easily achieved in India, the spirit phenomenon fascinates a growing number of people, leading them to explore and try to understand its nature. Our invisible population is emerging from the shadows.

14. Voodoo

THE WORD "VOODOO," from the French *vaudou*, is usually associated with the act of getting rid of one's enemy by sticking pins in a candle-doll. Moreau de Saint-Méry, in his monumental work, *Description of the French Part of Saint-Domingue* has translated the word *vaudou* as "an all-powerful and supernatural being."

Voodoo is actually a many-faceted conglomerate of African cultism and Catholicism. The slaves, transported to Haiti from Africa, retained their old beliefs and added to them the ideas of the Catholic missionaries. Voodoo is the main religion of Haiti, but it is also practiced in Brazil, other islands, and parts of the southern United States.

God and the Loa

The teachings by the Catholic missionary movement of one God, Jesus Christ, the Virgin, and the saints were easily accepted by the followers of vaudou and combined with their native beliefs. In Voodoo, however, God is impersonal and far off, like fate or nature, while the *loa* are nearby, sometimes dwelling in trees. The loa, also called "mysteries," are the beings worshiped by the followers of Voodoo. In the north of Haiti, they are called "saints and angels."

The loa are not the only supernatural powers worshiped in Voodoo. The Twins, who are extremely important, and the Dead, are among those who insist upon sacrifices and offerings.

The Voodooists believe that the loa were created by the "Great Master" to be of service to mankind, and they find daily proof of the loas' many kindnesses. There are also spirits who are willing to assist villains and to perform cruel and violent acts, but these are called "diab" or devils and are not contacted by the more upright Voodooists.

Adepts of Voodoo are not confused by the incompatibility of their polytheistic system and the concept of an all-powerful God. The loa are "like spirits, something like winds." They are like sons taught by their father, who remember the father's teachings even after leaving home. God is said to have taught the loa the same things which he taught the angels, but they revolted. Now, when they enter people, they possess them just as the Holy Ghost enters into the parish priest when he sings the Mass.

The following profession of faith from a Haitian peasant, recorded by Alfred Métraux in his book *Voodoo in Haiti,* expresses much of what the Voodooists expect from the loa:

> The loa love us, protect us, and guard us. They tell us what is happening to our relations who live far away, they suggest to us remedies which bring us relief when we are sick .... If we are hungry the loa appear to us in a dream and say: "Take courage: you will earn money" and the promised money comes.

An additional service of the loa, overlooked in this peasant's summary of expectations, as Métraux points out, is to warn his devotees of the machinations of those who wish to harm them.

Possession

In the Voodoo religion, the belief in possession is very strong. Those adept in Voodoo make a clear distinction between possession by loa, which is sought after and desired, and possession by evil spirits. In a ritualistic dance, a person may choose to come under a certain loa. Having then become unconscious of self, he can act out the part he has chosen. In the eyes of the spectators, the possessed person is not an actor, but the character itself.

The royal family of Abomey still worship a possessing entity known as Agassu. When Agassu possesses a person, he is forced to stiffen his hands and fingers into claws. Agassu was produced by the union of a panther and a woman.

Rada and Petro Gods

The Rada and Petro are two types of gods who are worshiped by the followers of voodoo.

The name Rada comes from the town of Rada in Dahomey, Africa. Rada gods and liturgy derive from the Dahomean religion. Petro rites, music, and divinities also originated in Africa. The name is associated with Pedro, a Spanish magician who practiced his magic on the natives of Haiti. He had a number of tricks and dances, including a dance similar to the voodoo dance. Don Pedro added a sprinkling of gunpowder to the rum being drunk by the dancers. The convulsive movements of the dancers, some of whom died, made a great impression on the spectators. Thus, the god Dompedre is a powerful god who is greeted by a burst of gunpowder in the rites.

New gods, new divinities, and new ideas of supernatural powers are constantly being added to voodooism. It was in this manner that Don Pedro became a loa—one who split, as did the African gods, into several different divinities.

When a devotee is suddenly possessed by an unknown god who announces himself in a trance or dream, the devotee hastens to introduce this new power to other members. A new cult within the present group may be formed, and this man may become a *hungan* or *mambo*, which is similar to a priest.

Legba and Agwe

Legba acts as interpreter for the gods. No loa shows himself without Legba's permission. Care must be taken that Legba is never offended. Legba is master of the mystic barrier between men and spirits. He is the guardian of all gates and fences and the god of roads and paths. Many magic formulas begin with the words: "By thy power, Master of Crossroads."

Legba is represented as a feeble old man in rags. He has a pipe and a haversack slung over his shoulder. When a Voodooist receives a Legba and is possessed by him, he throws himself on the ground, struggles frantically, or lies motionless as if struck by lightning.

Agwe presides over the elements. He is invoked under the names, "Shell of the Sea," "Eel," and "Tadpole of the Pond." Possibly, he is a counterpart of Neptune.

Belief Concerning the Souls of Plants and Rain

In addition to the worship of the gods, the religion of

Voodoo includes an animistic belief in spirits which inhabit things found in nature. Plants, fields, and rain are all believed to have souls to which the follower of Voodoo must respond as faithfully as to his deities.

It is the *namh*, the soul or essence, in foodstuffs that is believed by Voodooists to make children grow. The namh of plants has a very personal meaning to Voodooists. When herbs are to be gathered, the herb doctors go at a time when the plants are asleep and touch them gently in order to avoid aggravating the namh. As they pull them up, they speak to the plants in a soft, gentle voice, saying, "Get up, get up, go and cure someone who is sick. I know you are asleep, but I need you." The doctor is careful to put a few pennies beside the main stem to pay the soul for the effort of producing the cure in the sick one. When a plant dies, its soul goes in search of a residence in something else that is growing.

When a woodcutter is about to cut down a tree, he gives it a few taps to warn the resident, the namh, to get out. To be on the safe side, he will recite a prayer and invoke the Holy Ghost.

The big mapous, the soul of a wicked plant, wanders along the roads at night.

Every field has its own spirit.

The soul of rain strengthens the soul of the earth, and this in turn works upon the soul of the plants. Rivers, lakes, and lagoons, all have individual souls.

The Cult of the Twins

Twins, or marassa, living and dead, are endowed with supernatural powers. Persons who have twins in their family or in their ancestry must, under pain of "chastisement," serve them offerings and sacrifices. Sometimes a hungan will find that a family which has been having a series of misfortunes has not been paying homage to twins in its distant ancestry. When this neglect is corrected, all will go well again. The twins are worshiped next to Legba in most parts of the country.

A family remembering its twins who are long dead will have three holes dug near the house. Into these holes, fresh bowls of food are set from time to time.

A special, annual feast is held in the *humfo*, or loa sanctuary, for twin worship by all the families who attend that humfo. This is sometimes done on the Saturday before Christmas. The animals sacrificed are often a speckled hen or a brown kid. After the bowls are set out, the rituals performed, and the hungan states that the twins are satisfied, the remnants are placed in a huge calabash and given to the small children of the village.

The Cult of the Dead

The dead are the third category of supernatural beings in the Voodoo religion. The funeral customs of Haiti are very complex. Included with the Catholic liturgy are many practices dictated by fear of ghosts. If the dead is someone holding rank in the religious life of the community, the funeral rites are especially elaborate and strictly observed.

The *dessunin* is a mysterious ritual which takes place under macabre circumstances. After a person ceases to breathe, the hungan is summoned. He orders the family and others present to stand apart from the body. He then crawls under the sheet, placing himself over the corpse. His purpose is to invoke the loa to come out of the deceased. He shakes his rattle and utters incantations. At the moment that the dessunin occurs, many Haitians claim to have seen the corpse raise its head and shoulders. Some observers say that the hungan pulls the corpse up by its arms to create this impression.

Before the loa is asked to leave the body, the hungan performs a strange ceremony. He brings a live chicken, from which he has taken a fluff of feathers, and places it in a small white pot with some hair from the head and body and parings of nails from the left hand and left foot of the dead person. Hair, body hair, and nail parings become the vehicles and symbolic matter of the soul. Whoever possesses these has power over the person from whom they are taken.

This pot is sealed and carefully kept by the family until the day it is burned in the sacred flames.

The soul of anyone in death becomes a loa. The talent of a musician or skill of a sailor are dismissed by the dessunin rite Talents belong to the gods.

The Zombi

Métraux, in his book *Voodo in Haiti*, says, "Zombi are people whose decease has been duly recorded, and whose burial has been witnessed, but who are found a few years later living with a boko (or sinister magician) in a state verging on idiocy."

It is generally believed that hungan know the secret of certain drugs that can induce a state of lethargy indistinguishable from death. The old Haitian Penal Code had this article:

Article 246

> Also to be termed intention to kill, by poisoning, is that use of substances whereby a person is not killed but is reduced to a state of lethargy, more or less prolonged, . . . if after the state of lethargy the person is buried, then the attempt will be called murder.

It is by this means that the Voodoo priests create the zombi. The Haitians believe that a zombi is a living corpse that the sorcerers have raised from the grave by passing a bottle containing the soul under the nose of the corpse. The soul in its container has been bought from the corpse washer.

A zombi remains in that misty zone which divides life from death. Usually but not always male, a zombi is the unspeaking servant of its owner.

A zombi is a beast of burden exploited without mercy by its master. It is fed meager, tasteless food. In addition to the day's work, the zombi must go to the neighbor's fields and steal grain by night, or remove the blooms from the neighbors' coffee plants and return to his master's fields to place the blooms on his plants.

If a zombi is ever fed one grain of salt, he will awaken, become furious at the master, run wildly about, kill the master, destroy his property, and claw wildly at the earth of his own grave.

The belief in the reality of the zombi is so strong that steps are taken to prevent a family member from ever becomung one. Normally, a person is killed a second time by injecting poison into him or firing a bullet into the temple. Whoever has the job of killing the dead the second time must stand behind him to avoid being recognized in the community.

He must also be prepared to stand against the sorcerer who has been cheated of his prey.

"Another way out," Métraux states, "is to bury the corpse face down, mouth against the earth, with a dagger in his hand so he may stab any sorcerer who disturbs his rest."

Sometimes the mouths of the dead are sewn up to prevent their answering if their names are called by a sorcerer intent on finding a new zombi.

Another preventive is to place an eyeless needle in the coffin, so that the dead will spend eons trying to thread it and will be so involved that he will not hear his name called.

Voodoo Séances

The séances held by the Voodoo priests and priestesses are much like shamanistic exercises. The principal draws apart from the people, sometimes for days, and goes through many long speeches, prayers, and incantations, until the god that is being evoked appears.

The purpose of conjuring a god is usually to gain some knowledge required by a member of the group or to uncover some hidden fact. Also, the manner of transacting business or the feasibility of a trip may be discussed through the priest when the god is contacted.

As in the case of the séance, the voices speak in different tones. Often several voices speak during a séance.

Some mambo or hungan put themselves into a trance and become "ridden" by the god evoked. At these times, they foretell the future or give admonitions and various bits of advice.

Casting of a Spell

The adherents of Voodoo have a healthy respect for the possible ability of anyone to kill other persons by casting a spell. The hungan may find out who is perpetrating such a murder and may then punish the culprit severely. The hungan not only punishes the individual, but requires the family to pay large sums for many years following the murder.

Instead of stabbing a doll, often a glass or bowl of water is used by the one who wishes to get rid of a rival or enemy. The sorcerer, or anyone using this black magic, can lure his victim to him through incantations. The victim's image is stabbed when it appears in the water. If the water reddens it signifies that the person is dead.

In certain areas of the United States, particularly the eastern coastline and the Appalachian Mountains, people use a similar approach to the image. When a person dies in a household, the mirrors are all turned to the wall or draped until after the burial. This is to prevent the dead from seeing himself, and to keep his ghost from haunting the house. These practices seem to have a relationship with the image in the water and the death spell.

The Snake Rite

The rite of admitting a new person to the Voodoo faith is known as the Snake Rite, and takes place in the dark of the night. Damballah-wedo, the snake, symbolized by a combination of two snake forms around a drum, will not give of its power except through a priest or priestess.

The priest and priestess gather at the altar and make a long speech to the serpent in the cage. The priestess is placed prone at the top of the snake's cage. She begins to writhe and contort as she is penetrated by the god. During these contortions, she delivers an oracle. The snake is then placed on the altar and all the supplicants offer food and other sacrifices. Then starts the *danse vaudou*. This is the moment when the new members are received into the sect. They are in a trance from which they do not emerge until they are struck by the priest on the head with his hand, a wooden spoon, or a bull whip.

The ceremony ends with what Saint-Méry terms a "collective delirium." He explains that this state must result from magnetic emanations and that non-natives who are watching the dance rites are often struck with paroxysms similar to those of the participants, who may tremble from head to foot, then fall into a dead faint.

Charms and Amulets

Amulets, known as *gad*, offer protection for those of the Voodoo faith. An alligator tooth is soaked in a special potion composed of gunpowder and Shrove Tuesday ashes, bile of bullock and goat, water from a tannery, alligator flesh, and other substances. This broth, called potpourri or migan, is efficacious for one year.

Charm lamps are used for special protection. These are prepared by the priest known as *maman-loa* and are made from a coconut or crab shell containing oil on which two bone splinters float in the shape of a cross. Charm lamps can also be used in black magic to harm an enemy.

Vévé Drawings

Though idols and statues are not used to a great extent, Voodooists depend upon sybolic drawings, called *vévé*, to fulfill the function of a visual symbol to worship. The drawings themselves are believed to have magical power. As the hungan traces the vévé, he is causing the gods to draw near.

The vévé drawings are done with pinches of flour, powdered bark ashes, or coffee grounds. They are often scratched out in the earth and then filled in with the powder-like substances. These drawings, often quite large, can be done around the poteau-mitan, which is the center post of the area for the dance.

Voodoo Fulfills Its Followers

The mysterious and occult religion of Voodoo gives its followers the three consolations found in any religion: (1) remedy for ills, (2) satisfaction of needs, and (3) hope for survival.

Voodoo is a system which flourishes because it is eternally creative; the adepts continually enrich it with fresh contributions to both its mythology and its liturgy.

15. The Gypsies: Their Witchcraft

GYPSIES HAVE long been reputed to have special powers of divination and spells. Of all the people with power, they, more than most, are extremely fascinating. Their colorful costumes, haunting music, and elusive way of life evoke a sense of mystery and magic.

While gypsy tribes have long been known for their cunning and trickery, the power which is an integral part of the makeup and personality of true gypsies has enhanced their reputation for this special kind of wisdom. They have succeeded in spreading the ancient divinatory arts throughout Europe and into the United States.

Shamanism: The Roots of Gypsy Witchcraft

Mingled with gypsy wisdom are many superstitions and primitive fears. Gypsy witchcraft still contains some aspects of the ancient religion known as Shamanism. Shamanism was based on the belief that evil spirits were responsible for every unpleasant or tragic occurrence. Thus, the rites of the religion involved various forms of exorcism and benediction of these spirits. Poisons and human sacrifice were a part of the rituals of the more brutal Shamans. The voodoo practices of Africa and the West Indies derive from this cult and still contain many of its elements, such as the ceremonial dances and magic drums and chants.

Similarly, the witches of Tuscany have remained close to the practices of Shamanism. Many of their spells call for such revolting substances as bats' blood, frog bones, and dried flies.

Shamanism seems to have existed as early as Babylonian times. From there, its influence was felt in India and spread throughout Europe by the gypsies. The gypsies have distinctly Oriental roots; many words in the gypsy language are similar or identical to Hindi words, and many of the gypsy customs and beliefs parallel the practices of rural India.

Spirits, Giants, and Little People Forerunners of the Witches

The dominant personages of the gypsy religion are the spirits, as in the religion of rural India. Since the gypsies are an outdoor, wandering people, many of these spirits reside in nature, in such elemental things as wood, air, and water. The gypsies listen carefully to the babbling of the brook and the murmur of the wind, feeling in them a mystical presence which speaks of the rhythm of nature.

One group of spirits is known as the *Vile*. The Zcracne Vile are aerial spirits who play tricks on humans, often injuring them. They are also known to confuse men in the night and to lead them to unfamiliar places.

The Pozemne Vile are the earth spirits. These are benevolent spirits which are sought for their wise counsel. They are interested in the welfare of animals and teach gypsy women their secrets of medicine and sorcery.

The water spirits are known as Povodne Vile. These spirits are benevolent to men who meet them on land, but the man who meets them in the water is sure to drown.

Men have been known to seek the love of Vile women, for certain Vile women are said to be lucky marriage partners. A Vile woman, who is not immortal, will gain a soul by marrying a man who remains faithful to her.

Vile women are particularly attracted to a type of man called a *krstniki*. The krstniki is the youngest of twelve brothers, and his mission in life is to fight witches. On St. John's Eve, the witches have their greatest powers and they do battle with the krstniki, beating them with sticks and branches. In the autumn, gypsies and farmers in eastern Europe carefully clear from the land these things which the witches can use as weapons.

When a Vile woman is attracted to a krstniki, she invites him into her hollow tree. He visits for a period of time which seems like seven days. When he leaves, he realizes that seven years have actually passed.

Non-gypsies of Rumania often identify these Vile with witches. Perhaps this belief is associated with the very ancient idea that witches were wood sprites or fairies who lived inside hazel nuts. This concept gave the hazel tree its reputation for magical properties and inspired the term "witch hazel."

The Vile are not the only spirits which populate the gypsy countryside. There is a wood spirit named Panusch, whose amorous mischief suggests the Greek god Pan, and the malevolent Om Ren, who haunts the forest. Most dreaded of the forest spectres is Mashmurdálo, the meat-eater, who stalks the woods looking for men to devour.

The Water Man and Water Woman must also be conciliated. A gypsy who fills his jug in the stream must be careful not to draw water against the current for fear of offending the Water Woman. After drawing the water, he must spill a few drops on the ground as an offering to her. Her male counterpart, Water Man, lurks in deep pools of water, threatening the lives of swimmers.

An unusual group of "little people" is referred to by the gypsies as the "small men." These are gray-bearded dwarfs dressed as miners, who are concerned with the welfare of human miners. It is said that when a miner dies at his work, these dwarfs will knock three times at the door of the miner's home to notify his family. They may be heard quarreling among themselves and hitting one another with their axes or blowing their horns as a sign of battle. The seven dwarfs of the Snow White fairy tale bear a strong resemblance to these small miners.

The mountain monk is a mischievous spirit who delights in kicking over water pails, putting out lamps, and other foolish pranks. Sometimes he has been known to strangle workmen whom he dislikes, but at other times he helps miners by filling their lamps or guiding them when they are lost. If they tell of his help, however, they suffer for it.

Gana is queen of the witches and corresponds to the Roman Diana. Like Diana, she is a huntress and is followed by witches and fairies as she goes in search of prey. A powerful enchantress, she ruled all of Transylvania until the advent of Christianity. She is similar to the cat goddesses of the Norsemen and Turks. Diana and Herodias, who steals children, are worshiped by the witches of Italy.

The Dschuma is a fierce old witch, the embodiment of disease. She goes about naked and cold, and may be heard wailing in the night when there is an epidemic of disease. The gypsy women make garments for her and hang them out to pacify her and drive the disease away.

Rumanian gypsies also believe in house spirits. If captured, these spirits become slaves for seven years. In return, they receive the first mouthful of every dish which their master eats. This belief derives from the Hindus, whose house spirits provide food for their masters.

Belief in the various kinds of spirits preceded the actual practice of witchcraft. From the lore of the spirits' magic, the gypsies developed charms and spells. Some of the gypsies became witches who invested themselves with the magic which had been associated with the little people. The witches of their imagination acquired the powers of flight and transformation which are common to witches of all cultures.

Legends of Child Stealing

Gypsies have been known to steal children; Lilith, the legendary mother of witchcraft, also stole children. The oldest form of witchcraft involves disease as a form of child stealing. This idea is personified in Herodias, the child stealer whose daughters were fevers. Jews of earlier centuries believed in the Bennmerinnen, witches who haunt women in childbirth, as well as in Lilith.

It is believed that the reason gypsies stole children was the desire to have among them, for luck, a child who had been baptized.

There is a Rumanian legend which tells of the Archangel Gabriel meeting a witch who was on her way to steal children. She explained that she could enter houses by changing herself into a cat or fly or other animal form, but anyone who knew her twelve and a half names could not be touched by her. This legend was possibly the origin of the well-known Rumpelstiltskin fairy tale, which describes how a gnome spun straw into gold for a young woman. In return, she would have to give him her first-born unless she could guess his name.

The elves were also said to steal children, substituting their own children in place of the ones they had taken. It is from this idea that we find the word "changeling," used to describe a child who is mysterious or unlike the rest of the family.

Names for Gypsy Witches

The various names that are used for witches are interesting because they show how the concept of witches differs from one region to another. The English word "witch" comes from the Anglo-Saxon *wicca*, deriving from a root meaning "wisdom." The pure Slavonian *vjestica* and Bulgarian *vjesirica*, as well as the New Slovenish *veda* carry the same meaning.

Dalmatian witches are known as *krstaca*, which means "the crossed," or *rogulja*, which means "the horned" because of their association with the Devil. The Slovenes and Kai-Croats sometimes use the term *copernica*, but this is insulting to a witch. Anyone who uses this term invites the witches' wrath. The more acceptable word is *hmana zena*, which means "common woman."

The Hungarian witch is known as *cohalyi*, which means "wise woman" or *gule romni*, which means "sweet or charming woman." The more powerful witches, actually female magicians, are known as *lace romni* or good women.

The true gypsy word for witch is *chovhani* or in English gypsy, *chorihani*.

The Powers of a Gypsy Witch

A gypsy witch acquires her powers easily. Some say that the seventh daughter in each family is born with these powers. Thus, many gypsies claim to be seventh daughters in order to make their divinations more respected.

A witch may also receive her powers from another witch. It is said that a witch may not die until she has passed her power on to someone else. A story is told among Italian gypsies of a girl who inadvertently became a witch. The girl was a patient sharing a hospital room with the witch, a very old woman who was seriously ill but could not die. As the old woman tossed and turned, she cried in anguish, "To whom shall I leave it?" Thinking that the old woman meant money, the girl replied, "Leave it to me. I am poor." At that moment, the woman died and the girl herself became a witch.

Some gypsies believe that a witch's power is as easily lost as it is acquired. A witch may lose her power if she sheds even a single drop of blood or if she is found out to be a witch.

Protection against Witches

The gypsies' strong belief in witches caused them to develop various forms of protection against the witches' spells. Many of these protections have been incorporated in various ways into the practices of other cultures.

A witch can herself be bewitched by a song; for once it begins, she must listen to it until the end. An interlaced pattern or confusing design bewilders a witch and stills her powers; this is why Persians make carpets with such intricate patterns. Braided cords are also considered an effective protection and are used in decoration for this purpose.

Garlic is an effective means of repelling witches. Leeks and onions, which are considered similar, are also offensive to witches; the three vegetables are used in many gypsy charms. The reputation of garlic as a protection persisted so strongly in Europe that many Europeans who came to America in the early part of this century would put small bags containing garlic cloves around the necks of their children. This amulet was meant as a protection against colds, fevers, and other diseases which were believed to be caused by bad spirits or the evil eye of a witch.

Planting a lime, or linden, tree in front of the house is another way to keep witches away. This tree is known to be the symbol of love in Christian as well as gypsy tradition.

The Italians have signs which they use to defy witches. In Naples, the gesture is the extended fore and middle fingers, identical to the "V" for victory" or "peace" sign. In Florence, the gesture of defiance is the thumb placed between the fore and middle fingers. The most common sign of all is used in many countries—the four fingers wrapped around the thumb. Sometimes a chant is repeated as well:

Witchy, witchy, I defy thee.
Four fingers round my thumb.
Let me quietly go by thee.

The Gathering of Witches

There are many beliefs among the gypsies concerning the places in which witches gather and the holidays on which they hold their ritual meetings. The gypsies also have ways by which they believe they can see witches in flight. Stories concerning these flights and the witches' gatherings are part of the gypsy lore.

At night, the witches become active and meet to dance and work spells. Traditionally, witches assemble on the holidays of St. John's Eve, St. George's Eve, Easter, and Christmas. On these days, farmers deck their cattle with garlands of leaves and flowers to protect them from the evil eye of the witches.

Those curious and daring enough to wish to catch a glimpse of the witches may do so on St. George's Day. To watch safely without being seen, a man must be up before sunrise, put on his clothes inside out, and place a square of green turf on his head. Thus, he becomes invisible while watching the witches return on their brooms and various steeds from the revelry of the previous night.

St. George's Day is also the time when the witches enter churches to steal the axle grease from the church belfry.. They steal sacramental bread and wine as well and use these substances to work their magic.

A favorite meeting place of witches is in the branches of forked trees, such as ash or walnut. Particularly favored are those trees whose branches grow in the shape of a trident. This form is suggestive of the trushul, or gypsy cross.

Whenever a wild wind is blowing, the witches come out to dance. They whirl and leap about with the motion of the wind. When they gather at the Sabbat, or ritual meeting, they dance, often naked, to the music of the tambourine, violin, and flute. Their partners are devils and various animal-forms of the Devil.

Witches also meet on the crossroads when the moon is full, and they sit and spin there throughout the night.

Witches' may easily be recognized by the four-toed footprints which they leave in the sand. Because many birds also make this type of print, gypsies claim that witches often take the shape of birds, particularly the peacock and the quail, which are considered evil omens.

Although many witches ride to their rendezvous on brooms, a witch may have a special halter which she can slip on a sleeping man to change him into an animal which she can ride through the night. In the morning, the man will have no recollection of his transformation. The noted folklorist Charles Godfrey Leland tells a story of such an occurrence:

> There was once a very thin tavern-keeper whose wife was very fat. One day, a gypsy woman told this man's fortune, saying, "Do you know why you are so slim while your wife is so fat? It is because she is a witch. Every Friday night while you are sleeping, she slips a magic halter over your head. You become a horse and she rides you far away, over mountains, hills, and woods to the witches gathering. Although you are not aware of these journeys, the ride is hard and you are wasting away."
>
> The next Friday night, the man pretended to sleep, but when his wife drew out the halter, he grabbed it from her and slipped it over her head. She instantly became a mare, which he mounted and rode to the witches' meeting. A witch, whom he recognized as his godmother, warned him to leave before the other witches became angry. After riding back to his home, he called a blacksmith to shoe the mare. Slipping the halter off her, she became a woman again, but the horseshoes remained fixed to her, for anything which is done to a witch in another form will always remain when she changes back to her human form. Thus, she was denounced as a witch and thrown into a pit of quicklime.

The Dangers of Meeting Witches

The gypsies are fearful of meeting witches and take precautions to avoid such a meeting. If such an encounter should occur by chance, certain rituals are performed to negate its dangers.

If anyone should accidentally meet an assembly of witches, he must cover his head, make the sign of the cross, and take three steps backward, then one step forward. By this means, he can escape the power of the witches' wrath.

In England, the custom is slightly more formal. If a gentleman intrudes upon witches while they are gossiping over their afternoon tea, he should protect himself by walking backward to his overcoat and cane. He must then turn and walk out to the street.

There is great danger in swimming in water where witches have swum. Anyone who swims in these places will drown and his body will never be recovered. The witches' pools are usually deep and clear, often with a dead cat floating on the surface.

Anyone who is unfortunate enough to pass the spot where witches are spinning by moonlight will be bewitched into a deep sleep. If a man even ventures to walk over a place where witches have been, he will go mad.

If a man should take in his hand anything from the garden fence which a witch has laid there, he will fall sick within the year. If he has played with the object, he will die.

Transmitting the Knowledge

One of the duties of the gypsies was to pass on the arts and beliefs of witchcrafts to future generations. Charles Godfrey Leland, the most knowledgeable collector of gypsy folklore, was chosen to receive and translate a manuscript known as the *Vangelo della-Streghe*, or *The Gospel of the Witches*. The manuscript was presented to him by the Florentine witch Maddalena, who is greatly revered by modern witches.

This work contains the allegorical tale of Aradia, the daughter of Diana, the lady of darkness, and Lucifer, the light-bringer. Her mission on earth was to teach the secrets of witchcraft to mortals. She bestowed certain spiritual gifts on those whom she deemed worthy: to know success in love, to bless or curse with power friends and enemies, to converse with spirits, to find hidden treasures in ancient ruins, to conjure the spirits of priests who died leaving treasures, to understand the voice of the wind, to change water into wine, to divine with cards, to know the secrets of the hand, to cure diseases, to make those who are ugly beautiful, and to tame wild beasts.

These gifts, she felt, would enable the gypsy wisdom to survive.

16. The Gypsies: Their Charms and Spells

GYPSY MAGIC includes many charms and spells intended to conciliate the spirits and protect the welfare of the gypsy tribe. Many of these charms deal with the prevention of diseases or the encouragement of love, since these are the basic concerns of these wandering people. Here we also find traces of Shamanism as well as the common symbolisms that are known in many cultures.

Hungarian Scapegoat Rituals

An old ritual among the Hungarian gypsies and prevalent among many religions, involves a "scapegoat." To prevent disease within the tribe, a wooden box is made on the Monday after Easter. Inside, on a cradle of two sticks, the ritual objects, mainly herbs, are placed. Everyone must touch this box, which is then wrapped in red and white wool to symbolize purification. The oldest person in the tribe carries it from tent to tent so that everyone may spit upon it. It is then left in a running stream, with all the diseases and problems of the tribe inside. It is believed that anyone who opens this box will bring upon himself all the miseries it contains.

The Hungarian gypsies also use a tree as a scapegoat. They spit into a hole in the tree to pass a fever from themselves into the tree.

The gypsies believe that the first person to enter a new home will soon die. Therefore, they will put a cat into the house before entering so that the "scapegoat" will receive this curse instead of a friend or family member.

Charms to Protect Animals

In the rural life of the gypsies, livestock is often essential to the welfare of the tribe. Therefore, certain rites are performed in order to ensure that the animals will not wander away or be stolen.

To keep swine from straying, a hole is dug in the turf, filled with salt and charcoal dust, and covered with earth. An incantation is pronounced over it:

> This is thine,
> Come not to us!
> I give thee what I can
> Oh Spirit of earth hear!
> Let not the thief go!
> We have three chains,
> Three very good fairies
> Who protect us.

If the swine find the hole and root it up, they will not be stolen or run away.

To protect cattle from theft, three drops of blood from the finger of a little child are made to fall on a piece of bread. This is given to the animal to eat, and the following words are chanted:

> I give three drops of blood
> To become young and good;
> Who steals thee to him
> Shall be blood and flesh dried up!
>
> When blood and blood
> Pass into thy belly,
> Fire and fire and great fire
> Shall devour and devour all
> Who will eat thee!

When a cat returns home after wandering away, it is swung three times by the tail to keep it from straying again. From this rite, we derive the expression: "Not enough room to swing a cat in" to describe a small room or house.

Gypsy Love Charms

Young people around the world have always been interested in finding ways to be more successful in attracting the sweetheart of their choice. The gypsies have many charms to aid them.

A man who is in love with a particular girl will give her grass to eat without her knowledge. This charm derives from the ancient custom of placing a blade of grass in the mouth as a sign of surrender. Since domestic animals eat grass, this is a way of showing subjugation to a master.

A girl may win the love of a man by burying his footprint under a willow tree and reciting over it:

> Many earths on earth there be,
> Whom I love my own shall be,
> Grow, grow willow tree!
> Sorrow none unto me!
> He the axe, I the helve,
> He the cock, I the hen,
> This, this (be as) I will!

It is lucky for love if one finds a key. Very old keys are valuable amulets. Those who carry them will learn secrets, penetrate mysteries, and succeed in whatever they undertake.

A man who finds a willow knot can make a charm by taking this knot in his mouth and reciting:

> I eat thy luck, I drink thy luck,
> Give me that luck of thine,
> Then thou shalt be mine.

He then hides the willow knot in the girl's bed if he can manage to do this without her knowledge.

Gypsies believe that one can spread love by transferring blood, perspiration, or hair onto the body of a person. To extinguish a person's love, his or her hair, blood, or saliva is burned.

When a gypsy finds a red ribbon, tape, or piece of wool, he picks it up and wishes for the love of someone. If he has no particular girl in mind, he wishes to find a sweetheart.

A man who takes a shoe which a girl has worn and carries it near his heart will cause her to fall painfully in love with him.

An apple, which is a symbol of wisdom, is lucky for love. A person who can slice an apple in two without cutting a seed will be fulfilled in love. On St. Andrew's Eve, a girl must take an apple from a widow without thanking her for it. She cuts it in two and eats one half before midnight and the other half after midnight. That night she will see her future husband in a dream.

If a lover proves faithless, the rejected one can take

revenge through this spell. He must light a candle at mid night and prick it three times with a needle while chanting.

Thrice the candle's broke by me,
Thrice thy heart shall broken be!

Gypsy "Streaking"

The 1974 fad of "streaking," or running naked through a public place, may actually have derived from a gypsy love spell. When the moon was full, a girl would run naked around a house or group of trees. If she could return without being seen, she would marry the man she loved.

Nakedness has often played a part in spells and witchcraft. An element of the debauchery of the witches' Sabbat, or ritual gatherings, was the tendency of the witches to perform the rituals and dances completely unclothed.

In parts of Rumania, gypsies believe strongly in a spirit who is always naked and needs new clothes every year. The inhabitants of the district make a suit of clothes for him, and lay it out on New Year's Eve in a place which the spirit is expected to visit.

In 1866 in Wallachia, six young people, all naked, ploughed a circle around their village to prevent cholera from entering.

Rumanian farmers hold the gypsies responsible for a drought, since the gypsy trade of brickmaking is favored by dry weather. To bring rain, the farmers take a gypsy girl, clothe her only in leaves and flowers, and bring her around the village so that everyone might pour water on her.

In the mid-nineteenth century, it was recorded that girls in certain northern cities of the United States would attempt to run naked around the block or a public square without being caught by the police. Perhaps they were attempting to work the old gypsy spell.

Moon Legends

Gypsies have a special affinity for the moon. One gypsy legend recalls that the sun wished to seduce his sister, the moon, and therefore had to wander after her. A similar legend tells of a wicked sorcerer who made the gypsy leader, known as Chen, marry his sister, Guin. Because of this, the gypsies, sometimes known as Chen-Guin, must always wander.

In ancient symbolism, the horned rays of the moon were regarded as related to the horns of an ox; thus a relationship existed between the moon and agriculture and fertility. The good luck which is associated with horseshoes and boars' tusks comes from their resemblance to the horned rays of the moon.

The use of horns to symbolize the moon is also found in Exodus 27:2 which describes the requirement for the building of altars: "And you shall make horns for it on its four corners; its horns shall be of one piece and you shall overlay it with bronze."

A gypsy woman who is expecting a child will not leave her tent by moonlight.

A child born during a full moon will make a happy marriage.

Witches and gypsies choose moonlight as the ideal time to cast their spells. Moon worship is ancient, probably originating in India, and is mentioned in the Book of Job as a forbidden practice.

Gypsy Herbs and Plants

Herbs and plants, which are symbolic in many cultures, are also a part of gypsy lore. The gypsies, who have always been a rural people, long ago learned the medicinal value of certain herbs and plants and endowed others with magical properties.

Saffron is known to Christians as well as to gypsies as a symbol of magic and love. This herb is characterized by a brilliant yellow color. The color of saffron is still used in the robes of certain cults, such as the International Society for Krishna Consciousness.

Saffron, known as *carcom* in Hebrew, is mentioned in the Old Testament in Song of Songs 4:13: "Your shoots are an orchard of pomegranates with all choicest fruits, henna with nard, nard and saffron . . . ."

A wash of well-water and saffron is used by the gypsies to cure pain in the eyes.

The elder tree has a ghostly reputation in the northern countries, where it is referred to as Lady Ellhorn or Lady Ellen. Before chopping down an elder tree, a peasant would kneel before it and pray: "Lady Ellhorn, give me of thy wood, and I will give thee of mine when it shall grow in the forest."

The country people would make little puppets of a piece of elder pith with half a bullet under them to make them pop up when thrown down. The Slovaks called them Pikuljk, a servant of the Evil One who does favors for men, but receives their souls in return.

Because the elder tree grows in lonely, gloomy places, it is associated with death. Twigs of elder are sometimes planted on graves; if they grow, this means that the deceased is happy.

Elder is hung before a stable door to ward off witchcraft. The bark from the elder is used in charms.

Peasants make wreaths of elder to wear on Walpurgisnacht. This is meant to enable them to see the witches riding through the air on their broomsticks, dragons, and goats to the Infernal Dance.

Straw Lore

Straw is significant as a symbol of emptiness or fruitlessness. In France, the breaking of a straw meant the breaking of a pact. Witches would make a man of straw and give him life.

To cure a toothache, the Transylvanian gypsies wind a barley straw around a stone which is thrown into a running stream while chanting:

> Oh, pain in my teeth,
> Trouble me not so greatly!
> Do not come to me,
> My mouth is not thy house.
> I love thee not at all,
> Stay thou away from me;
> When this straw is in the brook
> Go away into the water!

In some countries, tubes of straw were thought to be the homes of tiny fairies. Related to this is the gypsy practice of laying straws on the table in the full moonlight of a Saturday night and chanting:

> Straw, draw, crow caw,
> By my life I give thee law.

The straws are then supposed to become fairies and dance to the cawing of a crow, who will come to sit on the window ledge.

Egg Lore

Eggs are considered lucky by the gypsies and are often hung up in homes. Coconuts, which resemble eggs in shape, are lucky as gifts. An egg built into a new building protects it against witches.

The gypsies are careful to break up their eggshells after eating the egg. It is believed that if witches obtain unbroken eggshells, they will be able to change the shells into large boats. These boats can travel rapidly over great distances, but if they are not brought home by midnight, they will sink and the witches will drown. Charles Godfrey Leland's *Gypsy Sorcery and Fortunetelling* includes the following story:

> A gypsy girl asked another gypsy why eggshells must be broken. She was told:
>
> You must break the shell to bits
> for fear
> Lest the witches should make it a
>   boat, my dear.
> For over the sea away from home,
> Far by night the witches roam.
>
> The girl answered, "I don't see why the poor witches should not have boats as well as other people," and she threw her unbroken eggshell as far as she could, calling, "Witch—there is your boat!" The shell was caught by the wind and whirled away; then a voice cried, "Thank you!"
>
> Much later, the gypsy girl was stranded on an island with the water rising all around her. Just as the island was almost washed away, a white boat came along carrying a witch with her black cat and broom. She invited the girl to jump in and rowed her to shore. After they landed, the witch said, "Turn around three times to the right and look every time at the boat." She did so, and each time she turned, the boat grew smaller until it became an eggshell again. Then the witch sang:
>
> That is the shell you threw to me,
> Even a witch can grateful be!
>
> Then she vanished—cat, shell, broom, and all.

Salt Lore

Salt is another common item which has great symbolism. Salt is the symbol of life and therefore cannot be eaten by the Devil. This is illustrated by the German tale of a peasant who had a witch for a wife. The Devil invited them to supper, but all the dishes were without seasoning. The peasant, despite all nudges and hints to be quiet, kept calling out for salt. When it was finally brought, he exclaimed, "Thank God here is salt at last!" and the whole ghastly scene vanished.

Demons were known to lurk to the left; therefore salt is thrown over the left shoulder for good luck.

Salt should not be eaten before sowing a field, as it is a preservative and will keep the seed from growing.

A compact made over salt cannot be broken.

Holy water contains salt, which also represents immortality.

In some Eastern countries, salt is carried in a little bag as an amulet to preserve health.

If a girl will walk naked by the light of a full moon around a field or house, throwing a handful of salt behind her at every step, she will get the lover of her choice.

Salt is used in love philtres to make love endure.

The story of Lot's wife, who became a pillar of salt, demonstrates the ancient belief in the mystical properties of salt.

Hair Lore

Hair, as an integral part of a person, was endowed with magical properties by the gypsies. Hair can be used in spells against a person; therefore gypsies are careful to destroy cuttings from hair as well as clippings from nails.

Sleeping bareheaded in the moonlight may turn hair white or cause it to fall out.

Red hair is lucky; a red-haired child is prized highly among the dark gypsies. For easy childbirth, red hair is worn next to the skin during pregnancy.

If a bird works a man's hair into his nest, the man will suffer terribly until the hair is completely destroyed.

To keep her husband faithful, a woman must bind her hair with his three times when the moon is full.

A long hair hanging on a man's coat is a sign that he has been among the witches.

Knots of hair made by witches must not be disentangled.

Toad Lore

Gypsies often keep toads as pets and find them easy to tame. They also find the toad to be of assistance in telling fortunes.

The Persians' use of the toad to symbolize Ahriman, Prince of Darkness, caused the toad to become known as a symbol of the Devil. In many Romany dialects, the same word is used for both toad or frog and devil. The toad's ugly looks have given it a bad name in the mythology of all races.

An old silver ring with a toad carved in blood stone was formerly a lucky amulet.

A gypsy story tells of a child-witch who took the form of a toad: A man was walking through the woods when he stepped on a toad and crushed it. At that moment, he heard a scream from a nearby gypsy camp. Going to the camp, he saw a child who had just died. The child had marks on him as if he had been trampled. Horrified, the man realized that the child had been a witch inside the form of a toad.

Lucky and Unlucky Practices

The gypsies have an elaborate code of rituals to prevent bad luck. Certain practices are avoided on certain days in order not to offend the spirits. Some actions are unlucky whenever they occur.

It is unlucky to have someone tread on your shadow. The gypsies will work a spell to produce a headache in any who does this.

A whirlwind is to be avoided, as it is believed to be caused by a devil dancing with a witch. Anyone who approaches a whirlwind is carried off to hell.

It is dangerous to point at a rainbow or a thunderstorm.

Meeting a priest or nun in the morning brings bad luck. It is lucky to meet a gypsy or a woman of easy virtue.

It is also lucky to meet a woman carrying a full jug of water. Meeting a woman with an empty jug, however, brings bad luck.

On Tuesday, there should be no spinning, washing of hands, or combing of hair.

On Wednesday or Friday, no one should use a needle or scissors, bake bread, or sow flax.

On Thursday, there should be no spinning.

On Friday, no bargains should be concluded.

On Saturday, no one should wash.

On saints' days, no work should be done at all.

Since industrious activities and washing were forbidden on several days of the week, the gypsies easily earned a reputation for being lazy and dirty.

Amulets

Certain items are carried by the gypsies as amulets. A caul from the birth of a child is believed in many countries to have protective properties.

An old and curious knife is often carried as an amulet. Knives play a part in witchcraft and gypsy spells. In the Shamanistic rituals, special knives were used to kill the animals or humans to be sacrificed. In the more modified practices, a knife stuck into a table is supposed to go straight to the enemy's heart.

Maria Theresa silver dollars are considered magical by gypsies. When a baby is very ill, three of these coins are hidden under its clothes.

English gypsies regard a shoestring as a type of protection.

Nuts, particularly those which are heart-shaped, are carried as amulets by many gypsies. Nuts, which resemble seeds, are considered to represent life. Because a nutmeat is enclosed in a shell, it is associated with a casket; nuts were found in ancient graves.

Wrought-iron amulets with cabalistic signs represent some aspects of gypsy mythology. The following interpretations were made by gypsy folklore expert M. Kounavine:

Amulet A, used by gypsies in the Ural Mountains, represents the sun, moon, and stars, earth, and a serpent. It can serve as a symbol of the universe, with the serpent representing the evil of the world.

Amulet B, from Bessarabian gypsies, shows a man surrounded by a halo, aided by the moon and the stars, and armed with a sword and arrows. Below him is the horse and beside him is the serpent. This picture represents the conflict between the good and evil principles; Jandra (the good) against Auromori (the evil).

Amulet C, used by a Persian gypsy sorcerer, shows a gleaming star and serpent. It is called Baramy or Brama and symbolizes the gypsy proto-divinity.

Amulet D, obtained from burial places of southern Russian gypsies, shows a flaming pyre and some hieroglyphics. It may symbolize the prayer addressed to the divinity of fire.

Sharks' teeth and shells are particularly lucky charms. The sound of the sea, which can be heard in the conch, gives special powers to this type of shell.

Fortune-Telling and Trickery

There is an ancient gypsy method of fortune-telling which may have derived from the sound of the conch shell. Certain glasses or goblets, when tapped, would produce a ringing sound. With practice in tapping and blowing upon the glass, the gypsy could cause the sound to resemble a human voice, and would claim to hear mystical predictions and answers in it.

Although gypsies are known to demand of their customers to "cross my palm in silver" before telling a fortune, occasionally a gypsy will give a startlingly accurate prediction to a stranger, then vanish with no demand for payment.

In various parts of Europe, some gypsies used to practice an old trick known as the Great Sorcery. A gypsy would go to the home of someone known to have substantial wealth. Knowing that "enough is never enough," the gypsy would offer to double this person's wealth by performing a special magic spell. In order to work this magic, the victim was requested to place all of his valuables and money in a package and either place the package in the cellar or hide it under the bed. Then he was told to close his eyes and lie quite still, not speaking to anyone until nightfall. At that time, his worth was supposed to have doubled.

While the victim was lying immobile, the gypsy would substitute a worthless package for the valuables and disappear with his treasure. The Great Sorcery is not unlike the well-known con game in which the victim is asked to draw his life's savings from the bank as a sign of good faith in order to have a share in money which has been "found" by the con man.

The gullible may be duped by the gypsy and curse him;

the wise may separate the superstition from the power and find new meaning in many familiar practices.

Conclusion
The Intellectualization of the Occult

IN MANY CHAPTERS of this book, a change can be seen in the practices of the occult as they pass through the Age of Reason, the Machine Age, and the Space Age. Like religion or social custom, occult practices cannot help but be changed by progress.

The chapter on poltergeists shows how the early belief that demons were the cause of poltergeists has changed to the current belief in the psychokinetic ability of sensitive individuals. Psychokinesis has been brought into the realm of science, with the emergence of the field of parapsychology, and is being tested in laboratories with the same degree of precision that is accorded to any other scientific experiment.

Divination, formerly in the hands of witches and sorcerers, is now practiced in various forms by housewives, businessmen, and college students. The real power of divination is now believed to lie, not in the cards, the crystal ball, or the palm, but in the ESP, or extrasensory perception, of the diviner.

ESP, which includes telepathy, or mind reading, clairvoyance, or second sight, and precognition, or foreknowledge, is being tested in laboratories in the same manner as psychokinesis, which is actually a form of ESP.

The chapter on necromancy showed the development of the art of contacting the dead from the earliest sorcerers with their magic circles to present-day spiritualists and mediums. Here again, the practice of this art is no longer restricted to witches and warlocks. Mediums are tested systematically by scientists for evidence of fraud.

The current interest in the spirit world centers around the possibility of determining whether or not the soul lives after death. People who have "far memory," or the ability to recall previous lives in another body, are investigated to attempt to verify the details of their memories.

Astral projection, in which the "ghost" walks out of the living body, is also subject to scientific scrutiny. Individuals who can project themselves voluntarily are placed in controlled laboratory conditions to guard against the possibility of fraud. All the evidence is being weighed. One day science may be able to prove the existence of ghosts.

Even witches, who claim to be part of an ancient tradition, cannot help but be affected by the lifestyle of the twentieth century. Most modern witches are not followers of the Devil who are seeking material happiness, but are part of the wave of back-to-nature migrants who are reacting to an overly materialistic and overly-synthesized society. In reawakening their primeval instincts for ties with nature and close, communal affinity they are repudiating the anesthetized world of the Establishment.

Yet, the commercialization of witchcraft is another theme of the twentieth-century occult. Courses on witchcraft, which are easily filled to capacity, are offered in universities across the country. Mail-order courses are available which, for a substantial fee, claim to teach spells, meditation, divination, and any other skill a witch might need. The sale of witchcraft tools and related items, such as talismanic jewelry, is big business.

The Devil, which was represented in earlier times as a very physical and animal-like creature, has evolved into a suave, clever being who is less frightening than amusing. Although the movie *The Exorcist* has done much to reawaken the fear of the Devil, people have been known to laugh throughout the movie.

In general, the world of the occult has moved from the physical to the mental level. The emphasis has been on meditation and spiritual growth as a means of reaching the subliminal powers.

The world of the occult will not be conquered by scientists in a single leap. However, in the same way that the physical world has gradually yielded its secrets, the world of magic is growing more definable and more tractable. The time may come, many centuries in the future, when occult researchers may mourn with Alexander the Great that there are no more worlds left to conquer.

www.ingramcontent.com/pod-product-compliance
Lightning Source LLC
LaVergne TN
LVHW091632100826
845152LV00001B/7

* 9 7 8 0 8 2 4 6 0 1 9 0 4 *